AF473739

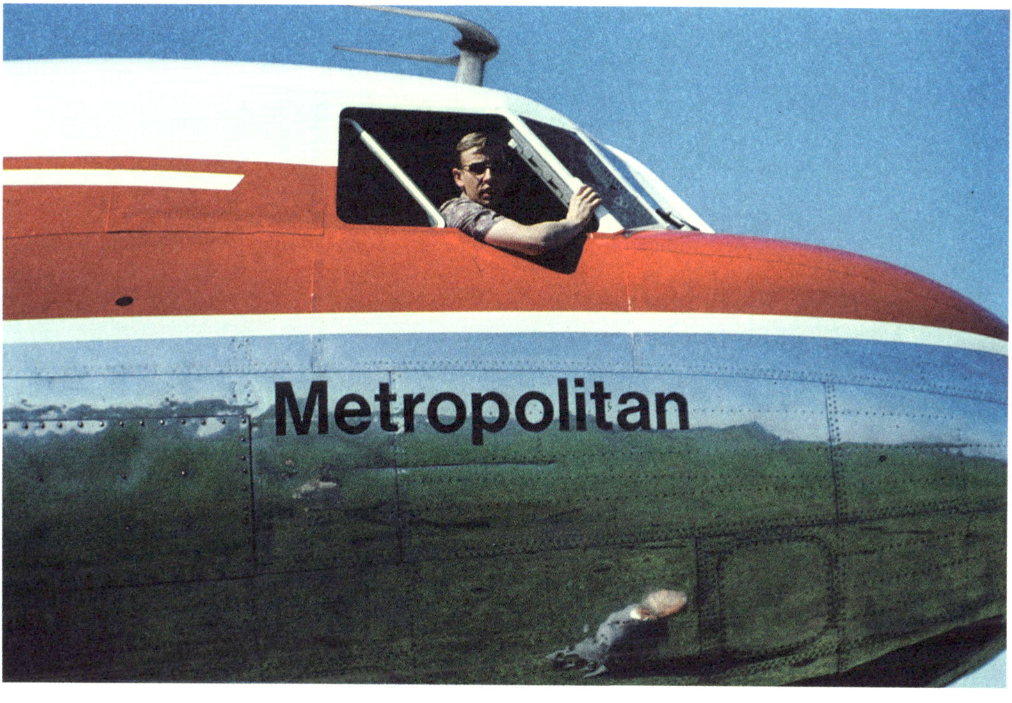

Metropolitan

Continental Breakfast

Axel Herrmann (1946–2010) begann 1967, sein aufregendes Leben als Verkehrspilot in Bildern festzuhalten. Auch wenn sein Beruf die Fliegerei war, so waren seine Leidenschaften die Fotografie, die Reisen und ab Anfang der 1970er-Jahre auch seine Frau Heide, eine Stewardess, die er kurz nach dem Beginn seiner Pilotenkarriere kennengelernt hatte. Bis 1979, dem Jahr der Geburt des Sohnes Daniel, führten Sie ein Jetset-Leben, wie es die Werbeagenturen der Zeit kaum besser hätten erfinden können. Der gut aussehende, unternehmungslustige Pilot und die attraktive Stewardess flogen zusammen um die Welt, zu den Sehnsuchtsorten jener Zeit wie London, Venedig, Hawaii, Tokio, New York, Rio de Janeiro, Bangkok, Hongkong … Während der damals noch langen Layover–Zeiten wohnten Sie in luxuriösen Hotels, mit Zeit für ausgedehnte Ausflüge, Badeurlaube und Sightseeing – lange bevor der moderne Massentourismus dem Reisen die Exklusivität nahm. Axel Herrmann hatte stets eine Kamera dabei und ein gutes Gespür für Situationen und den richtigen Moment. Die Farben des heute legendären Kodachrome-Umkehrfilmes lassen die privaten Erinnerungen auch nach fünf Jahrzehnten noch nostalgisch leuchten.

Die Bilder dokumentieren auch die große Liebesgeschichte zwischen Axel und Heide Herrmann, ob nun auf Reisen oder während der Heimataufenthalte, bei Familienfeiern und Festen. Er fotografierte sein Lieblingsmodell im Flugzeug, beim Arbeiten, vor Sehenswürdigkeiten, am Strand, am Pool, vor Sonnenuntergängen, im Hotel, mit Freunden und Verwandten. Die Bilder reflektieren zudem Axel Herrmanns Interesse an Technik – bevorzugt eine Boeing 747 – am alltäglichen Bordleben auf 30.000 Fuß Höhe, an den Flugroutinen während der langen Überseeflüge, die von Blicken aus dem Cockpit auf die Erdoberfläche unterbrochen werden. Nach dem Tod seiner Frau im Jahr 2002 vernichtete Axel Herrmann den größten Teil seines Film- und Fotomaterials. Auch die hier gezeigten Bilder wären fast verloren gegangen. Sein Sohn Daniel machte zu dieser Zeit seinen Abschluss an der HfG Offenbach und scannte für seine Diplomarbeit einen Teil des väterlichen Diaarchivs ein und edierte die Bilder unter dem Titel »Continental Breakfast«. Nur diese Scans und ca. 100 Originaldias sind erhalten geblieben. Seiner Arbeit ist es zu verdanken, dass es dieses Buch und die Ausstellung über das bemerkenswerte Leben seiner fliegenden Eltern überhaupt geben kann.

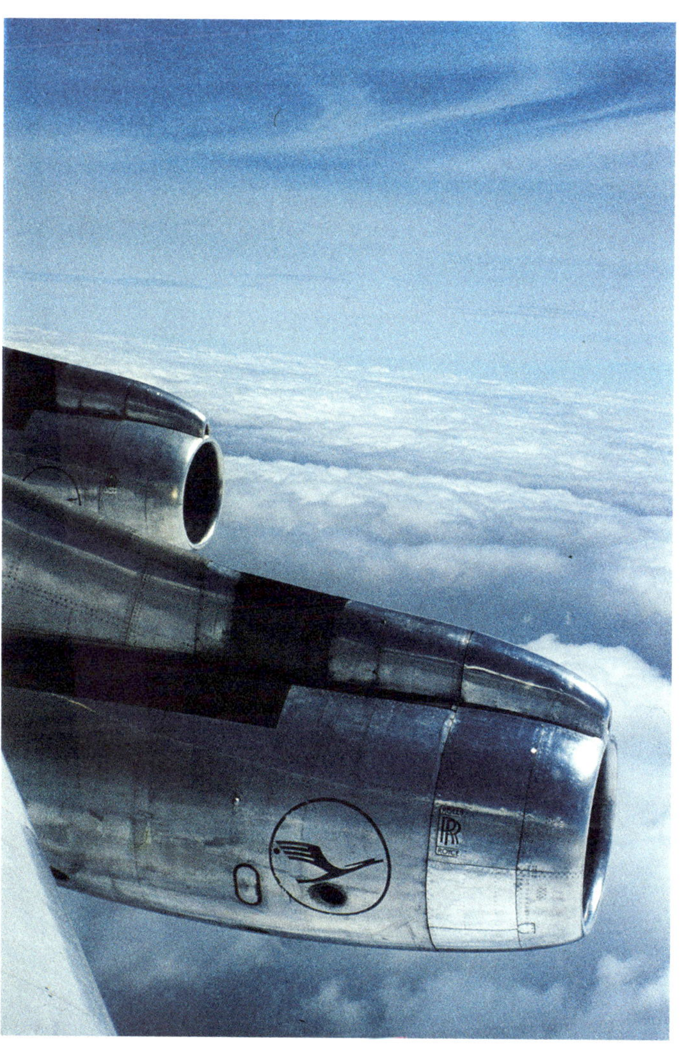

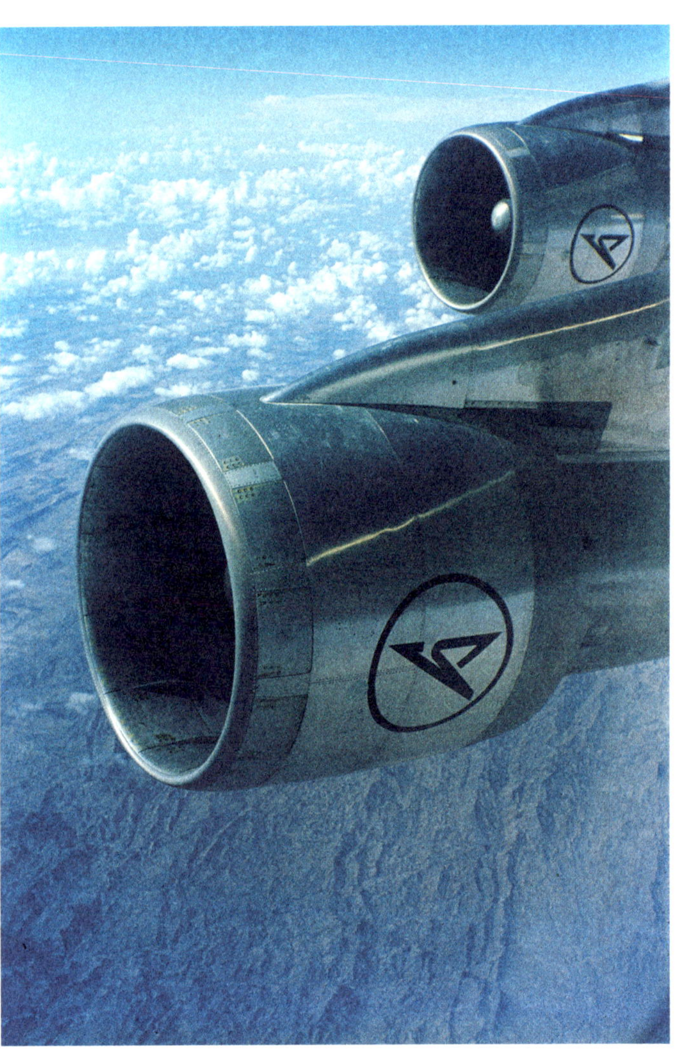

Continental Breakfast

Axel Herrmann (1946–2010) began documenting his exciting life as a commercial pilot in photographs in 1967. Although his occupation was flying, his passions were photography, traveling, and, starting in the early 1970s, his wife Heide, a stewardess whom he met shortly after beginning his career as a pilot. Until 1979, the year their son Daniel was born, they led the lives of jetsetters, in a way that the advertising agencies of the era could have hardly invented more authentically. The good-looking, adventuresome pilot and the attractive stewardess traveled around the world together, to faraway places like London, Venice, Hawaii, Tokyo, New York, Rio de Janeiro, Bangkok, and Hong Kong ... During the layovers, which back then were much longer than today, they stayed in luxurious hotels and had time for lengthy excursions, beach holidays, and sightseeing—long before modern mass tourism made traveling less exclusive. Axel Herrmann always had his camera with him and had a good sense for situations and the right moment. The colors of the now legendary Kodachrome reversal film allow the private memories to shine nostalgically even after five decades.

The images also document the great love between Axel and Heide Herrmann, whether they were traveling or at home in Germany or at family celebrations and parties. Axel photographed his favorite model in airplanes, working, in front of tourist attractions, on the beach, at the pool, against a sunset backdrop, in hotels, with friends and rela- tives. The images also reflect Axel Herrmann's interest in technology—especially Boeing 747s—including everyday life on board at thirty thousand feet and routine on the long-haul flights, in contrast with views from the cockpit of the earth's surface. After his wife's death in 2002, Axel Herrmann destroyed a large part of his film and photo material. The images shown here were also almost lost. However, Axel's son Daniel, who was doing his final project at the design school in Offenbach, scanned part of his father's slide archives and gave them the title "Continental Breakfast." Only these scans and around one hundred original slides have survived. His project made this book and the exhibition about the unusual life of his flying parents possible.

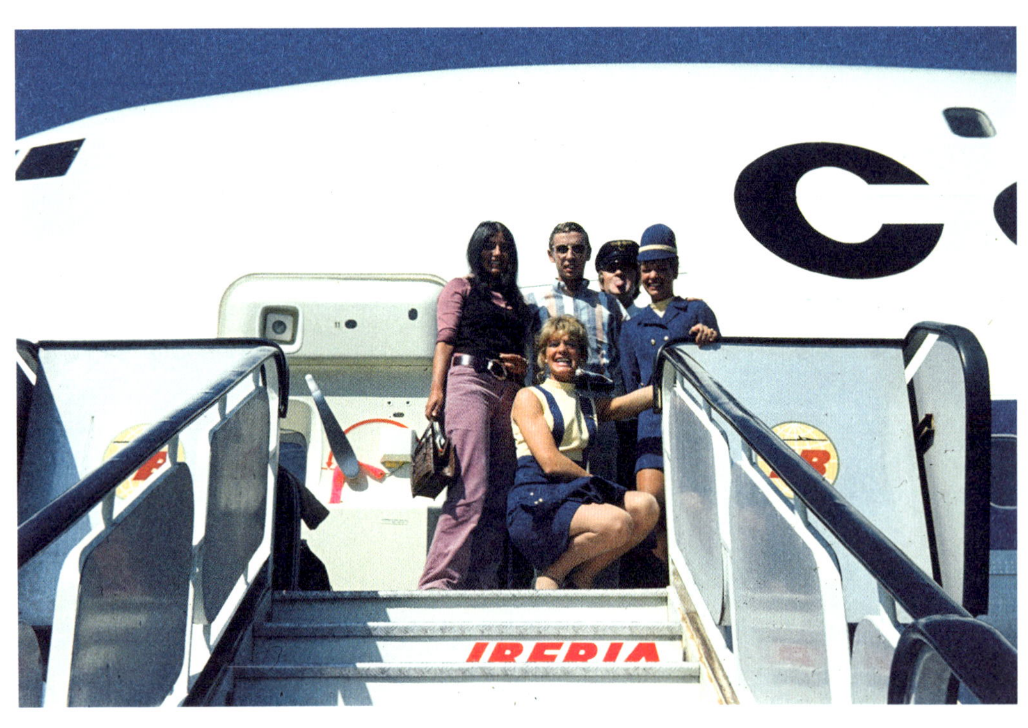
IBERIA

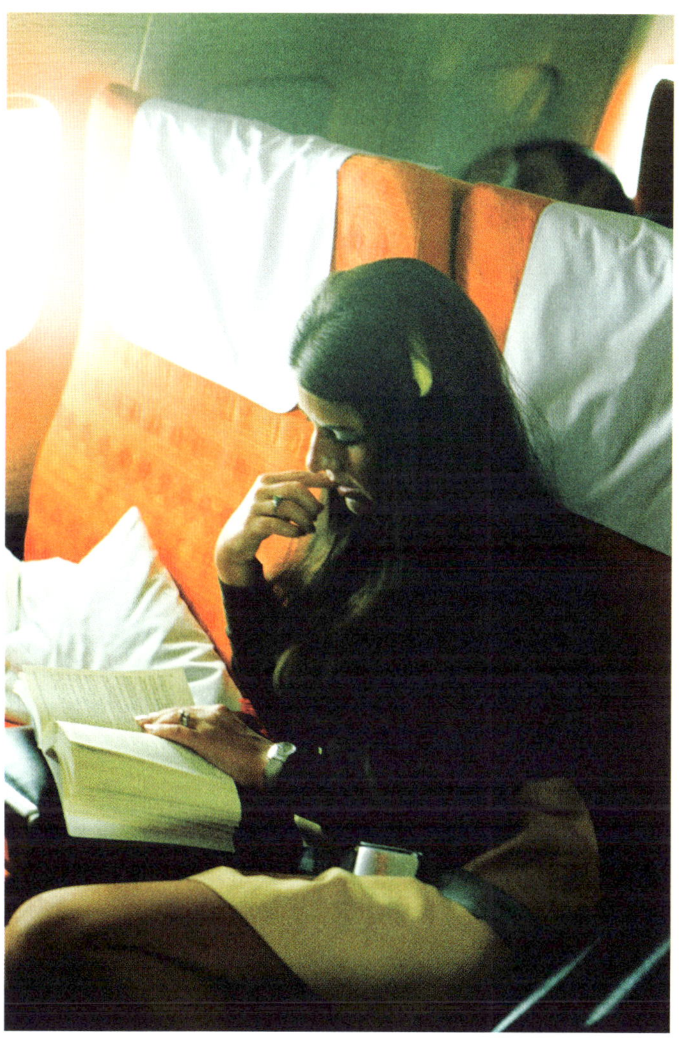

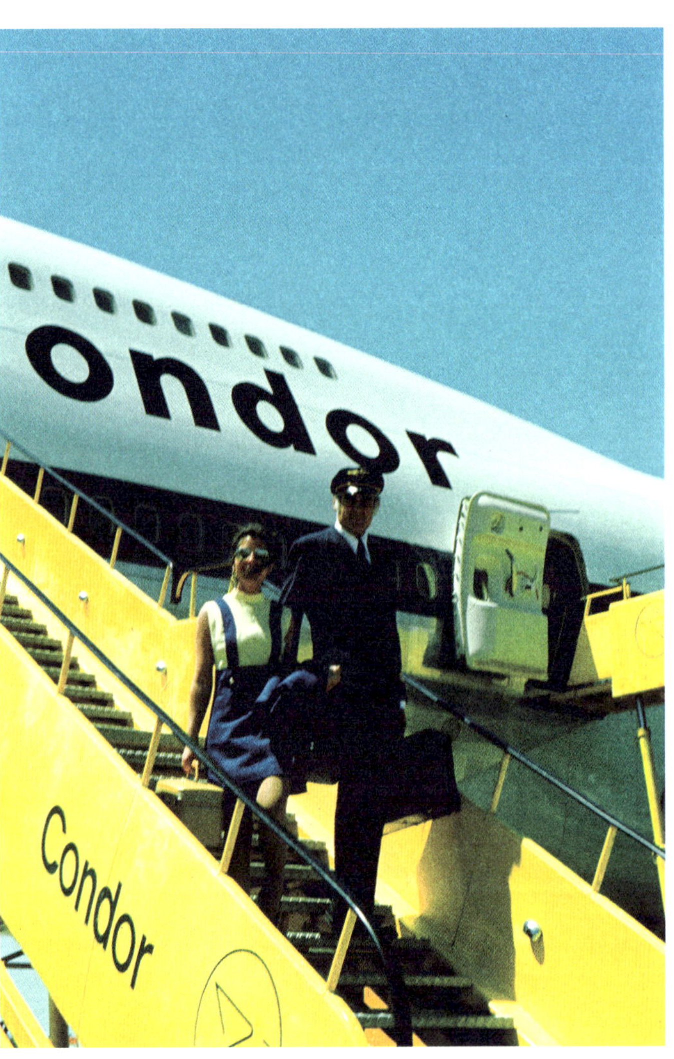
ondor
Condor

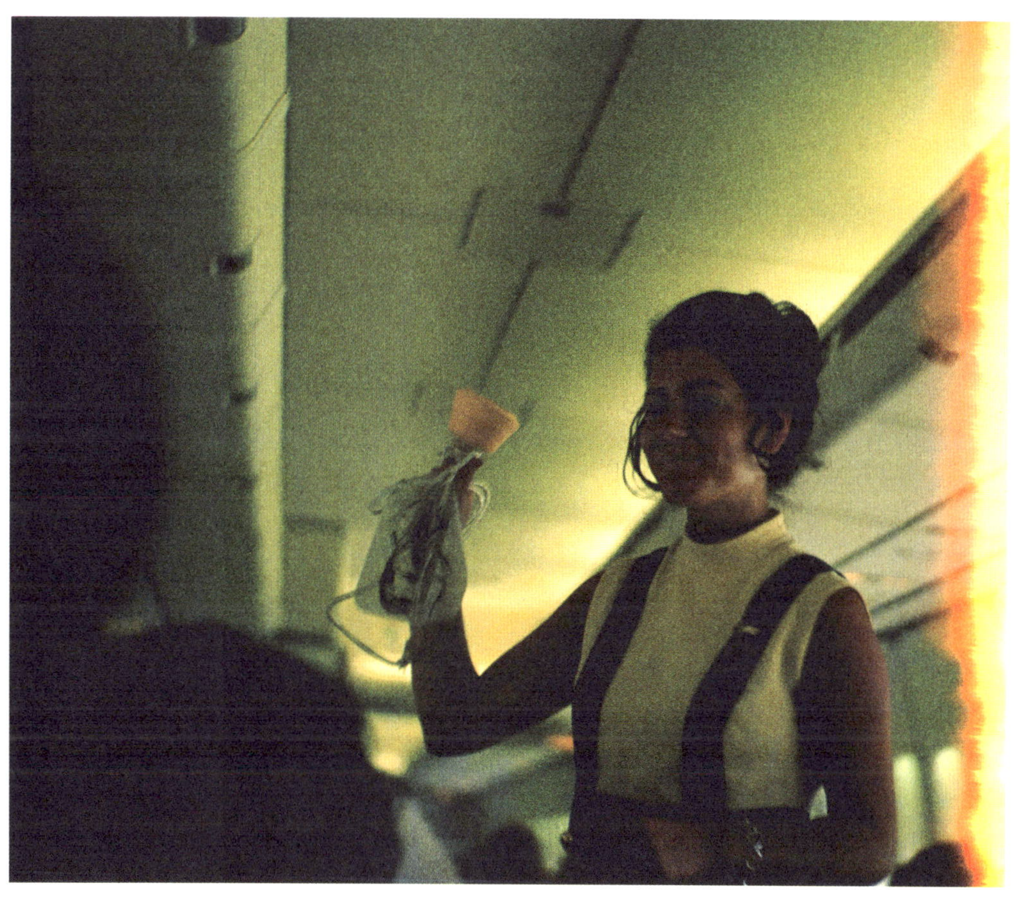

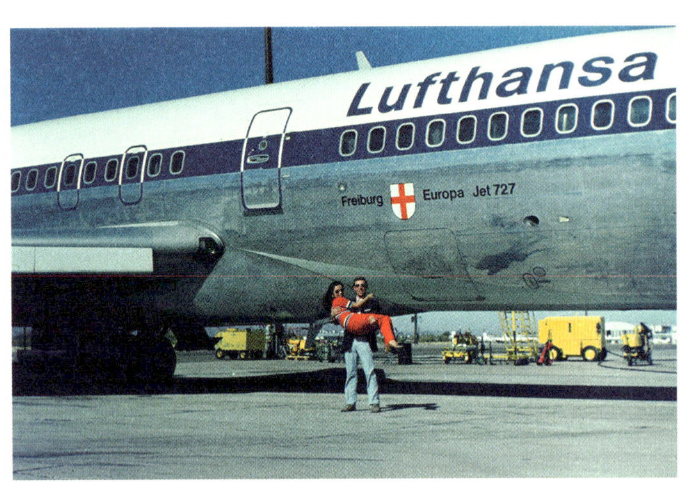
Lufthansa
Freiburg
Europa Jet 727

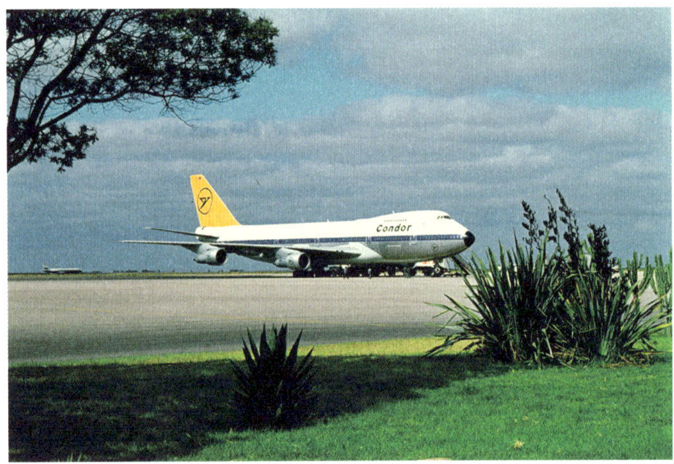
Condor

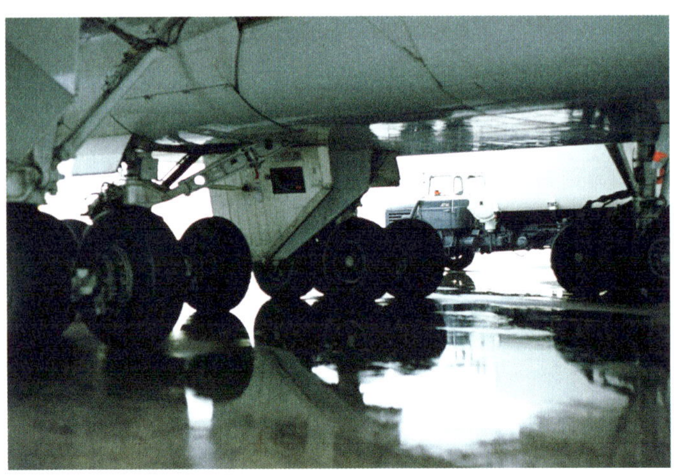

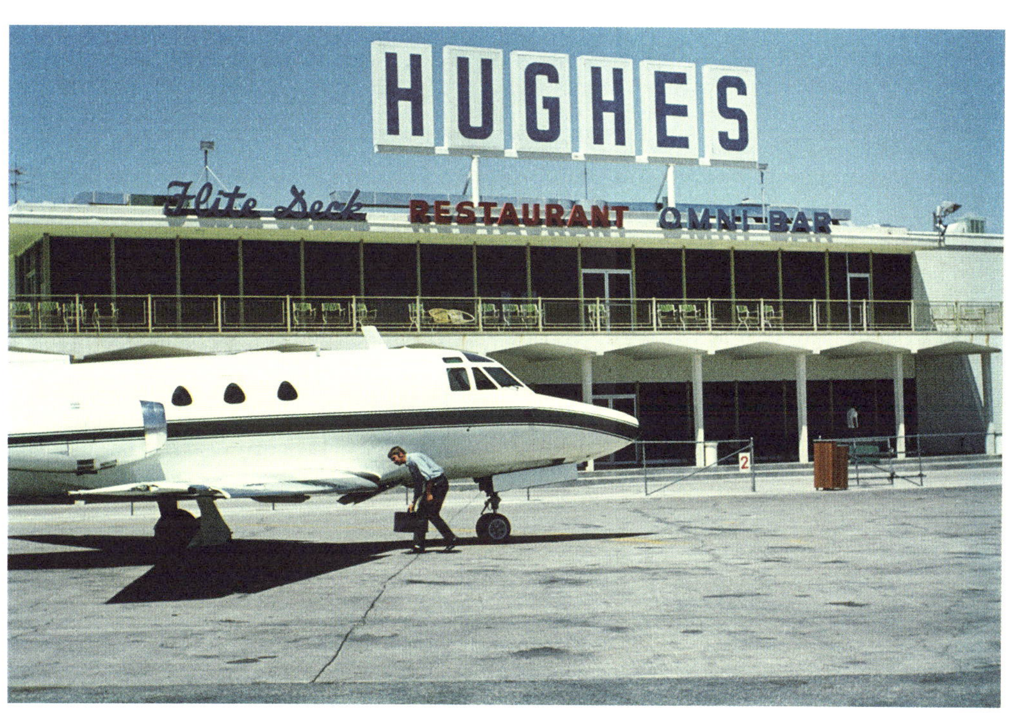
HUGHES
Flite Deck
RESTAURANT
OMNI-BAR
2

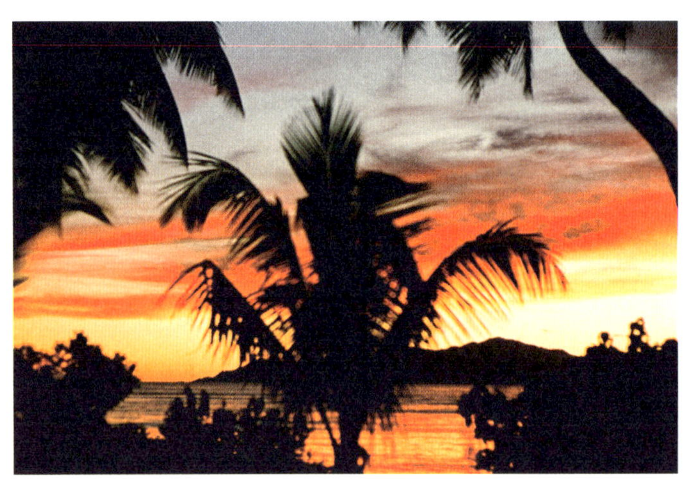

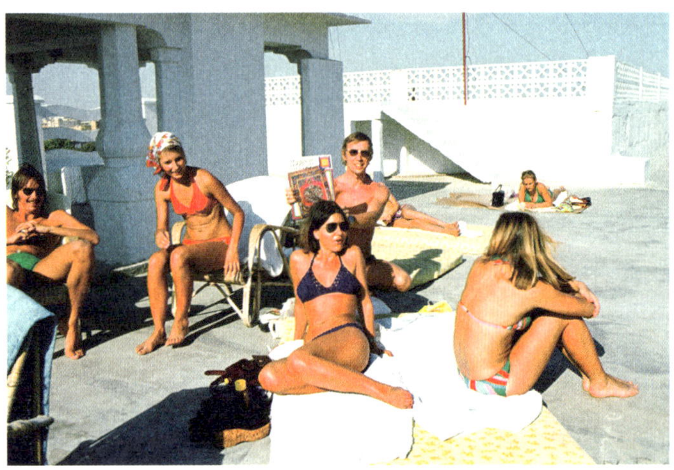

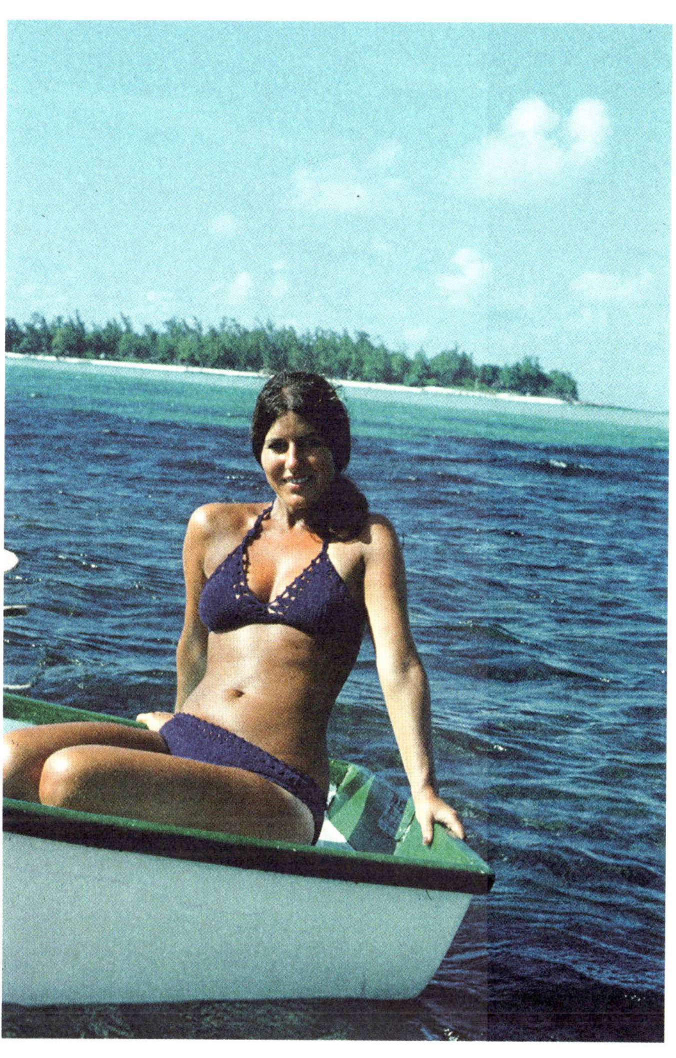

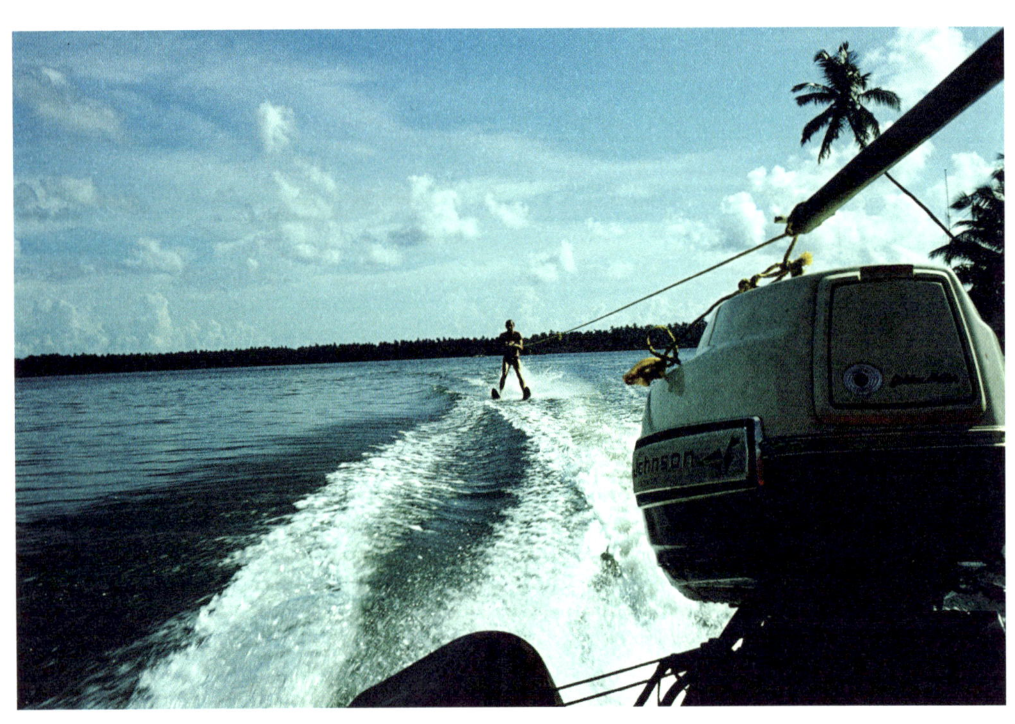

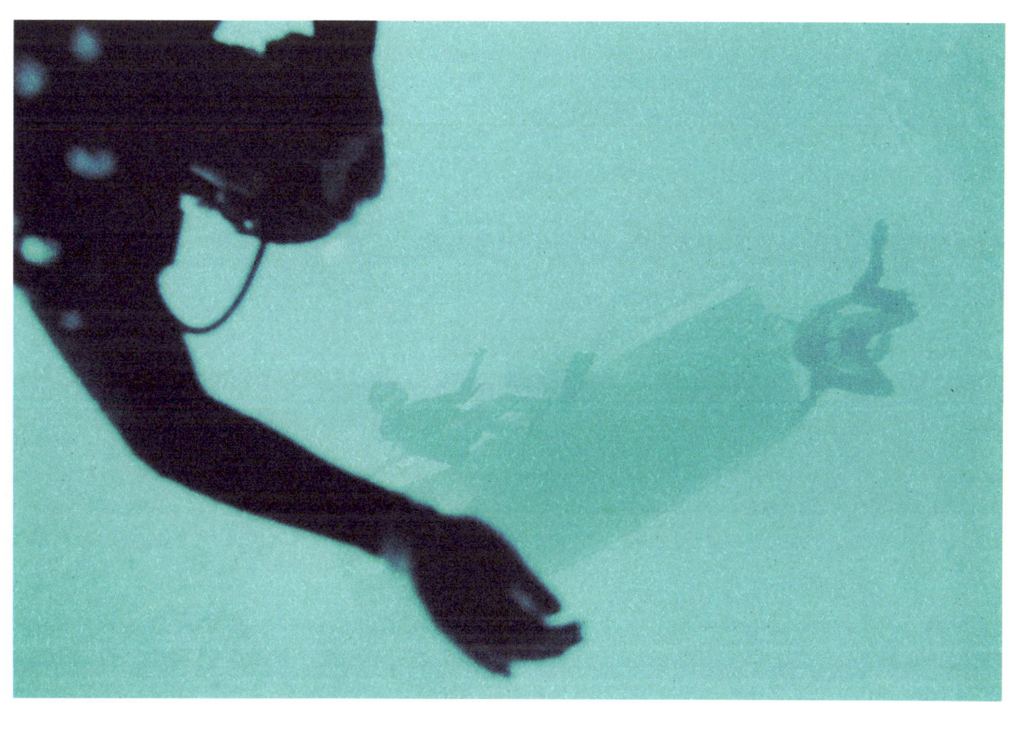

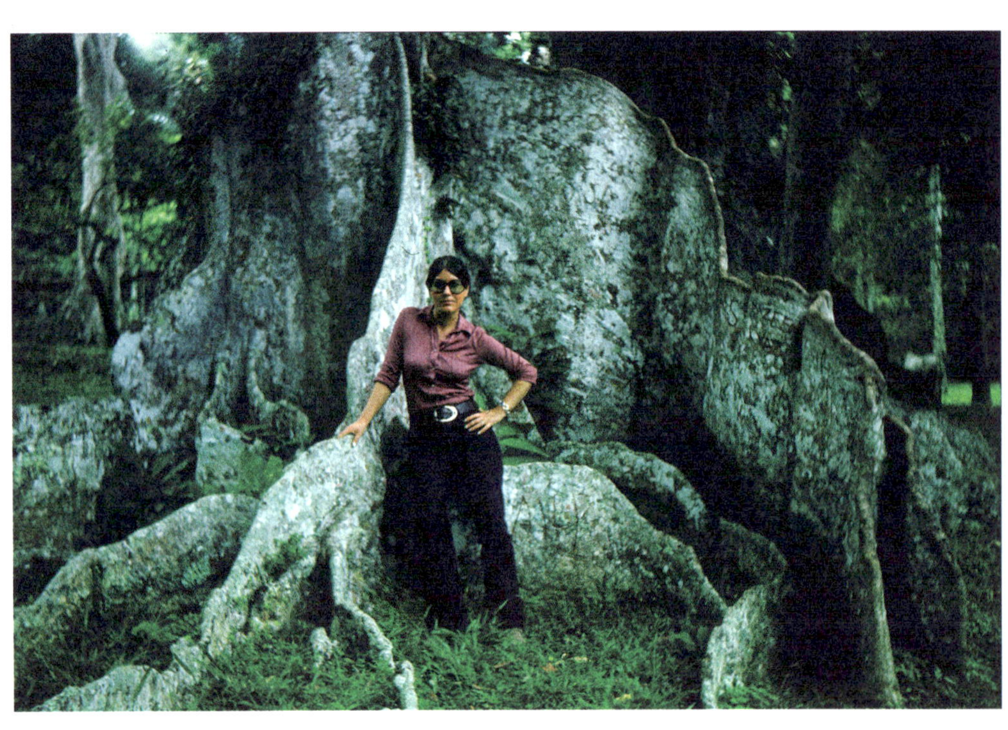

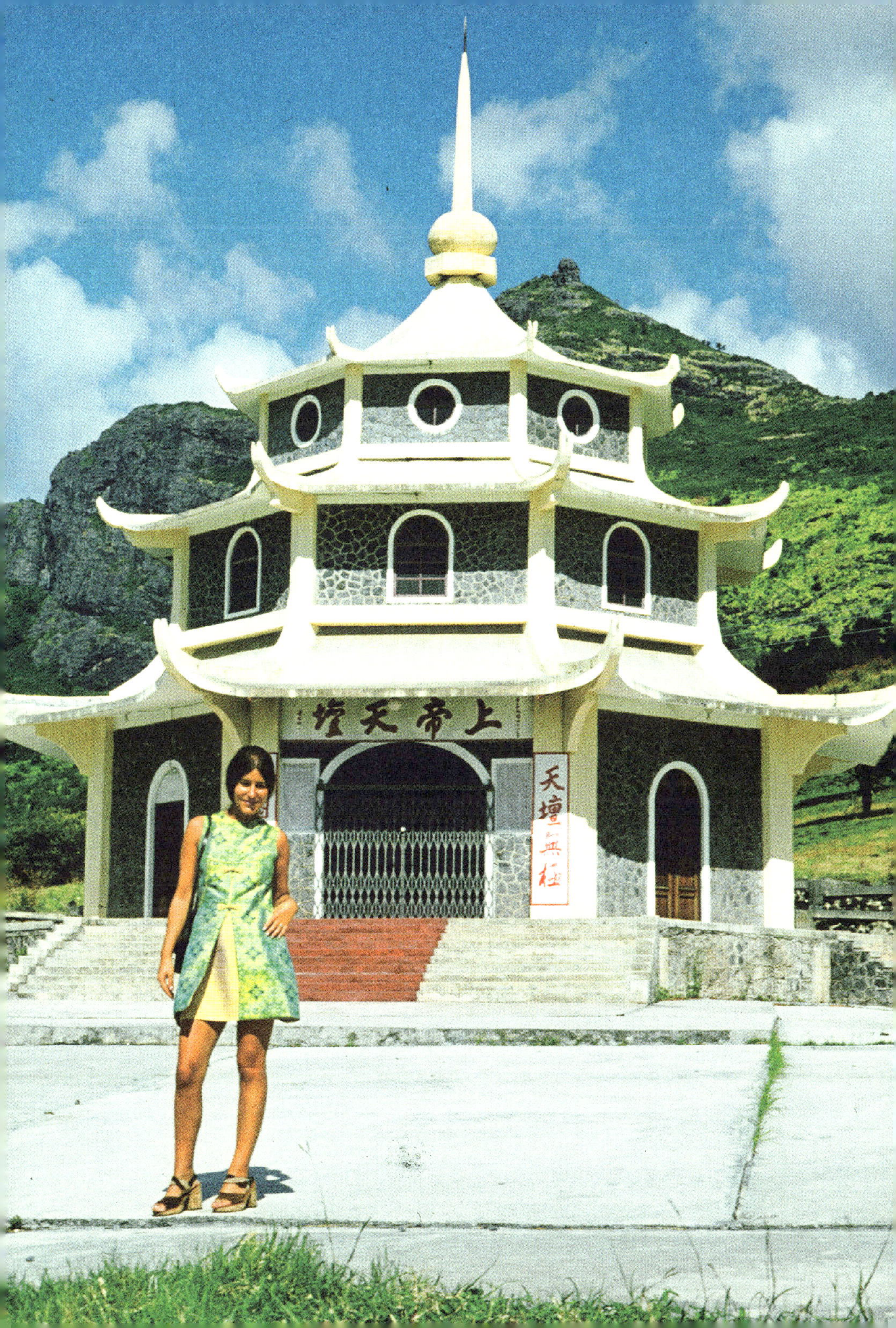
上帝天壇
天壇無極

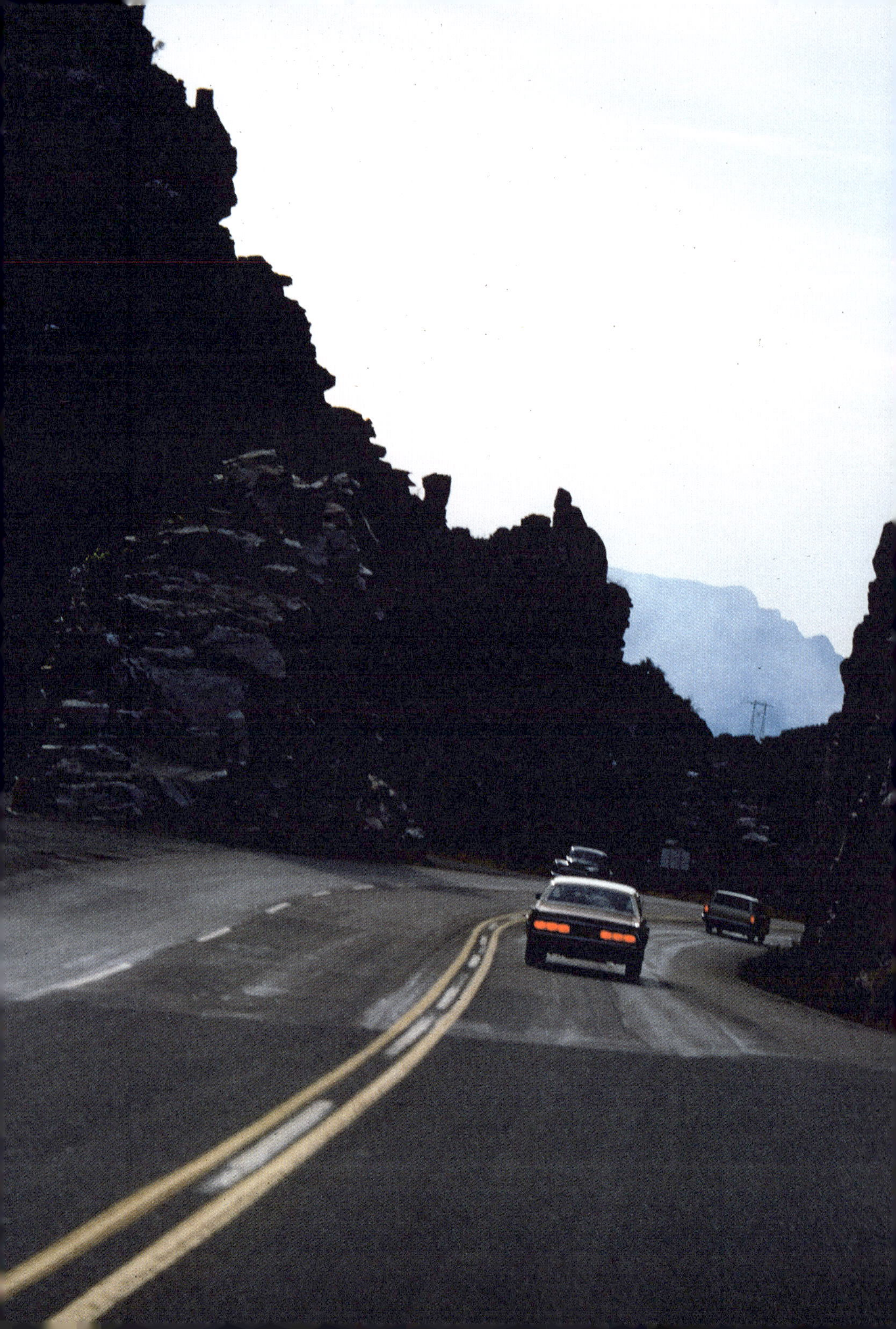

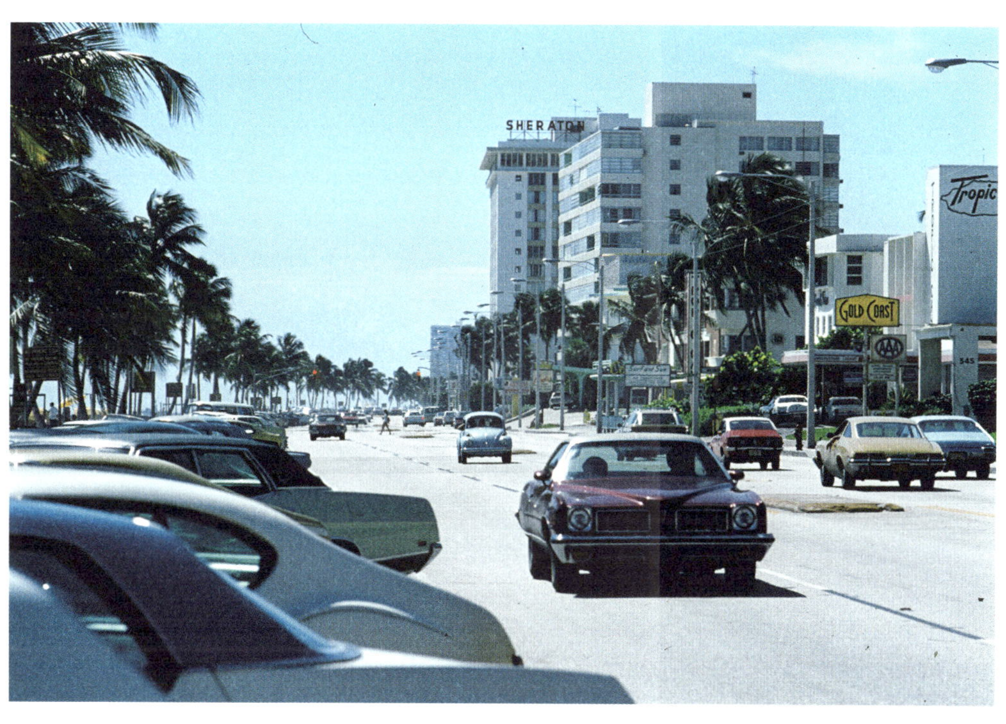
SHERATON
GOLD COAST
AAA
Tropic
545

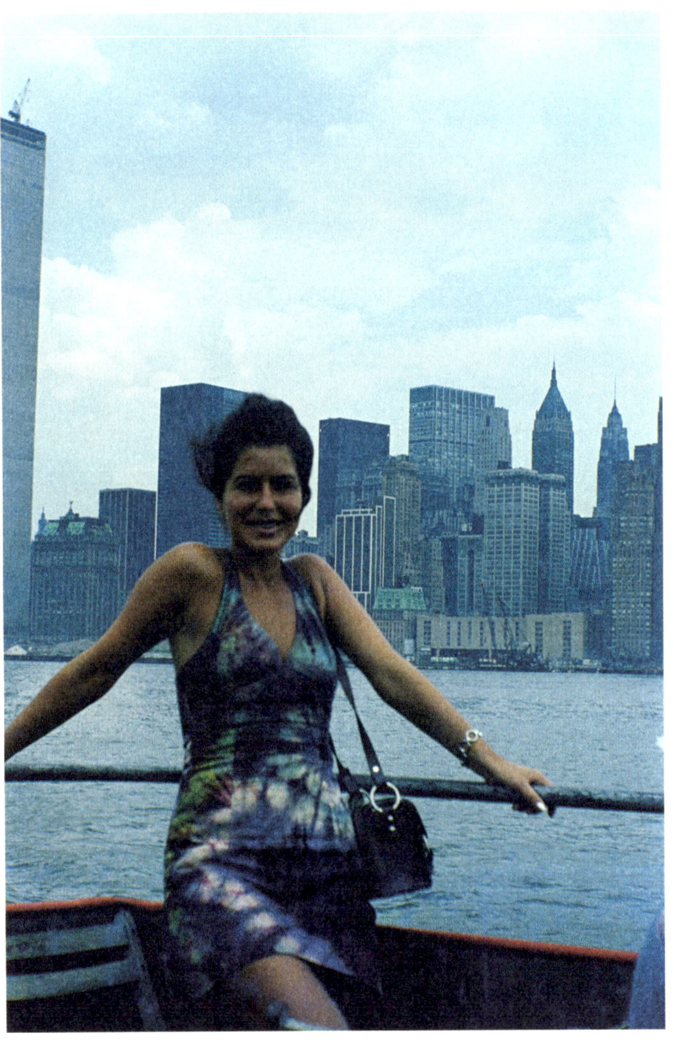

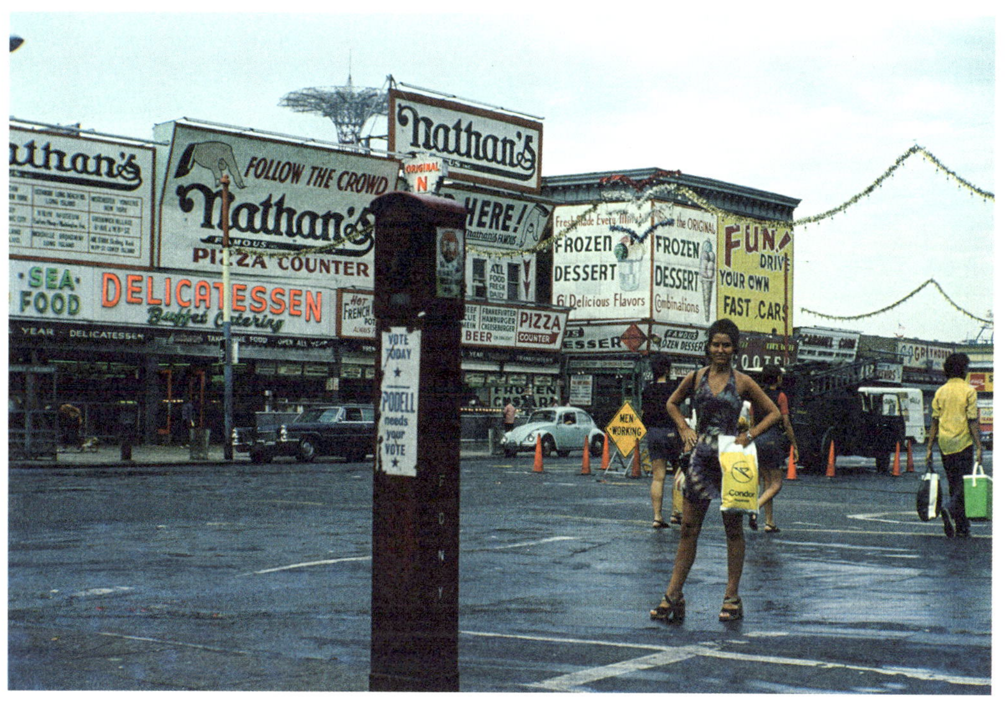

Nathan's
FOLLOW THE CROWD
Nathan's
PIZZA COUNTER
SEA FOOD
DELICATESSEN
Buffet Catering
ORIGINAL N
HERE!
FROZEN DESSERT
6 Delicious Flavors
the ORIGINAL FROZEN DESSERT Combinations
FUN! DRIVE YOUR OWN FAST CARS
PIZZA COUNTER
BEER
MEN WORKING
VOTE TODAY
PODELL needs your VOTE

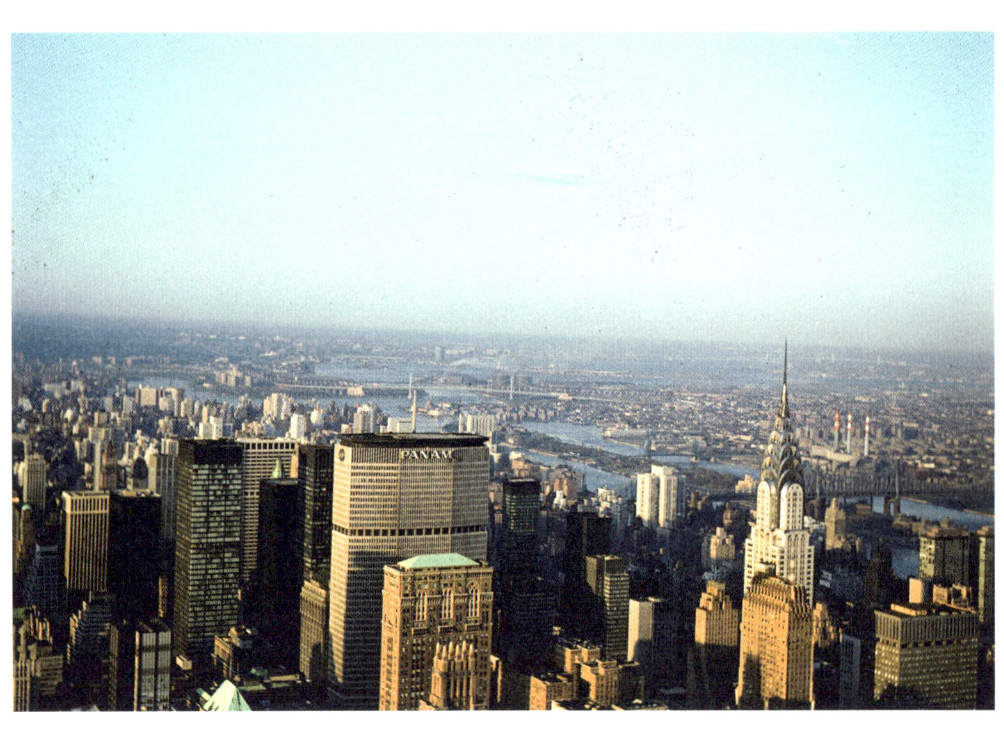
PAN AM

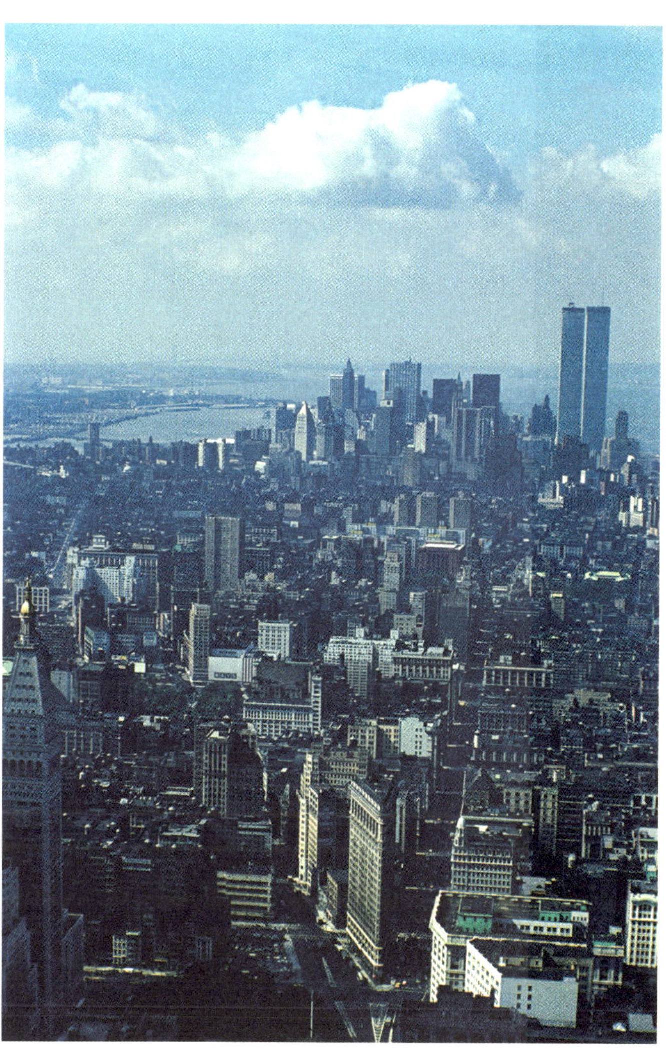

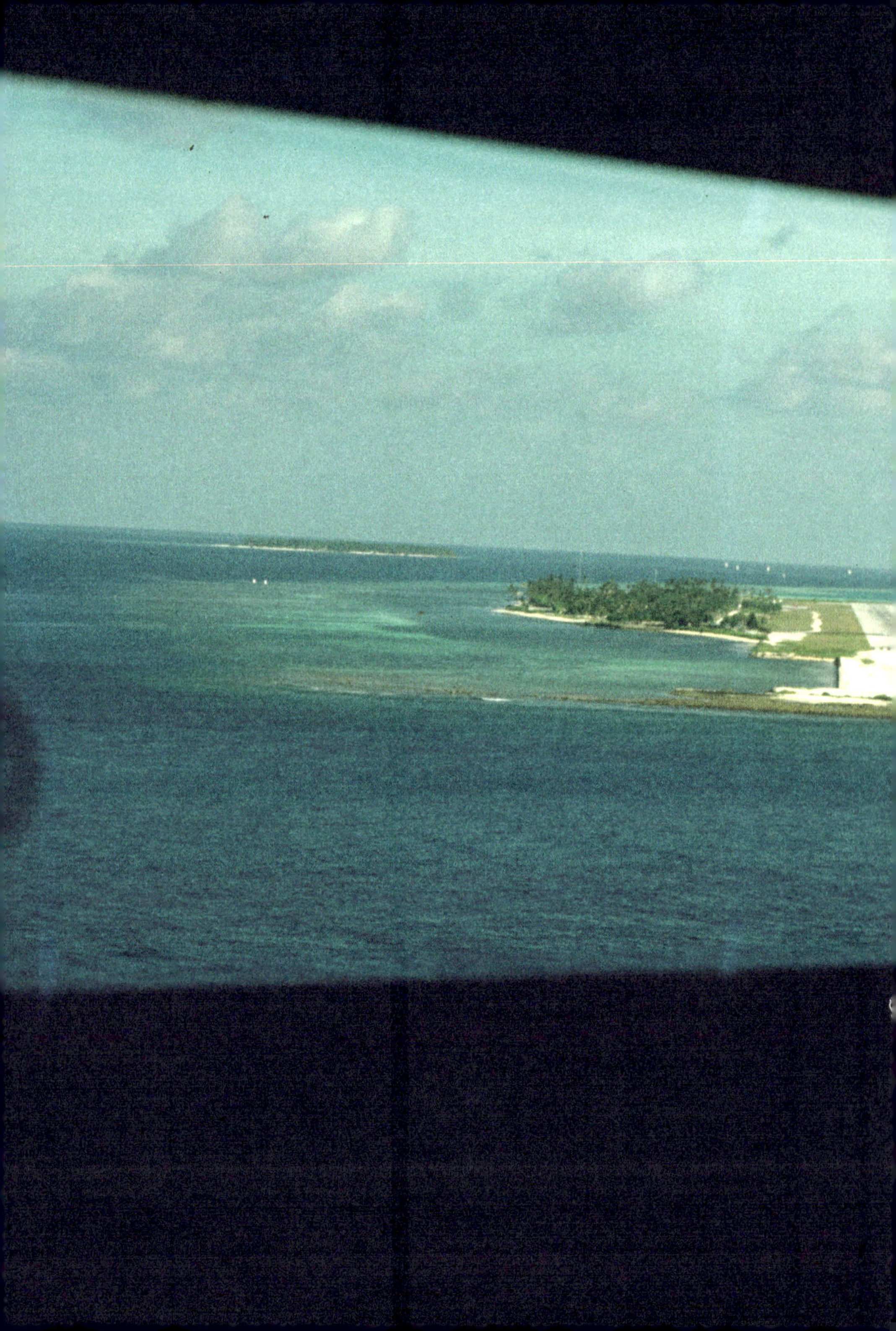

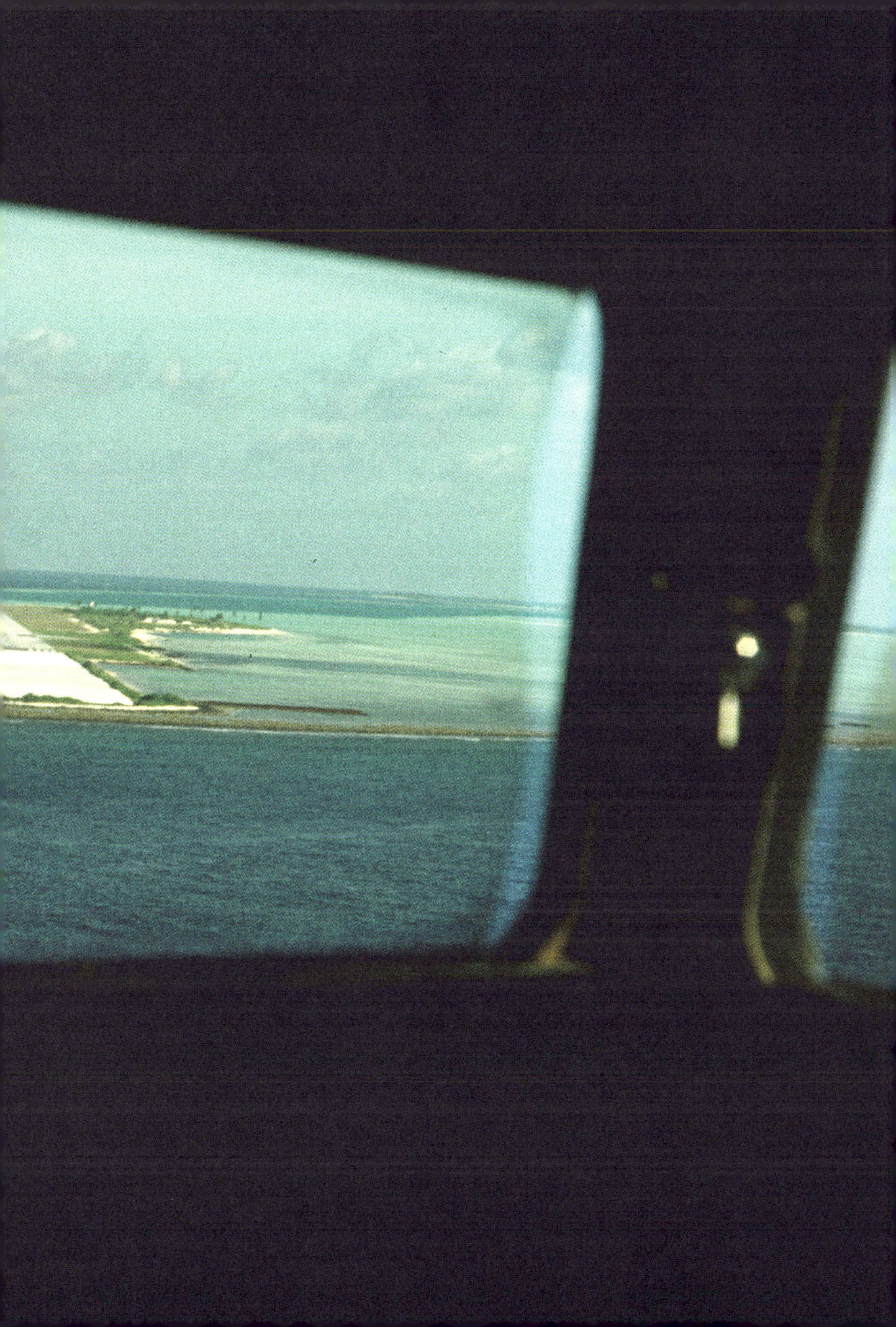

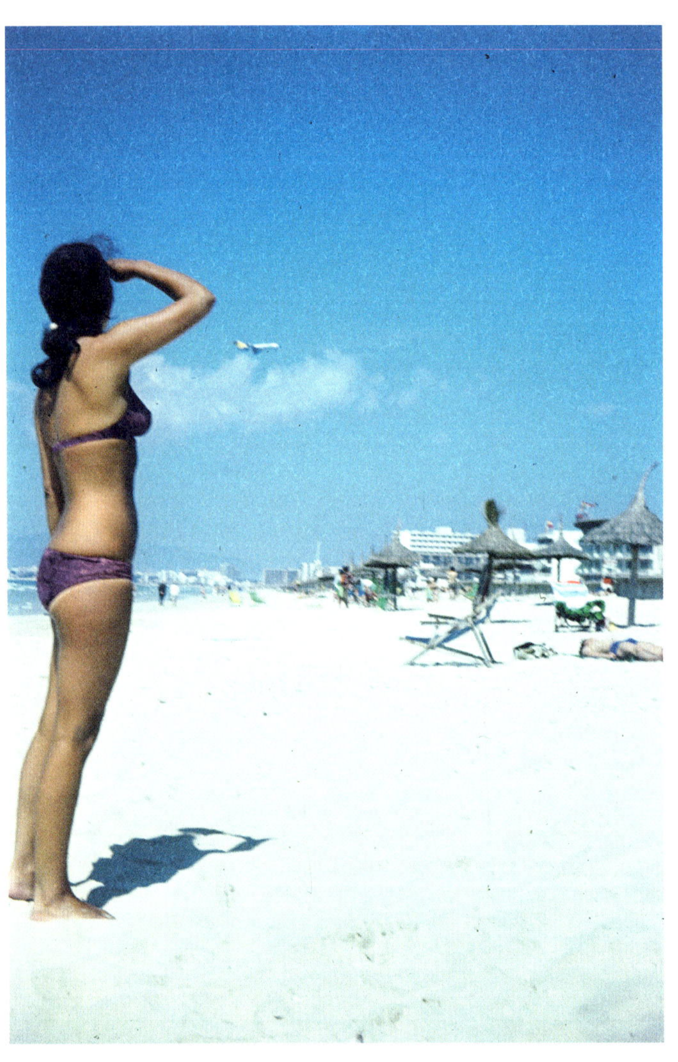

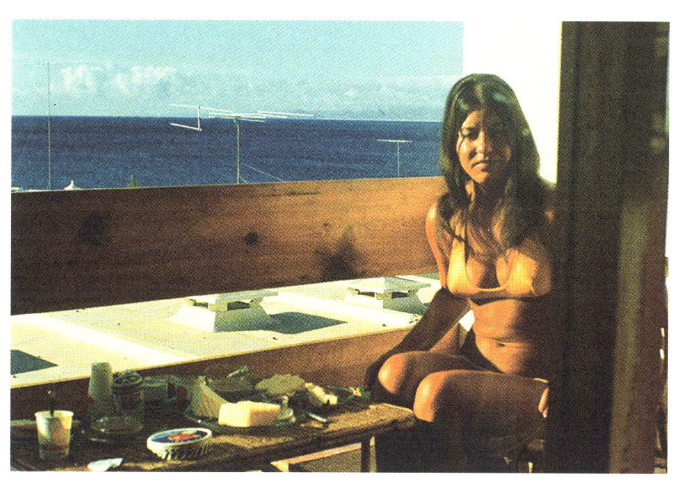

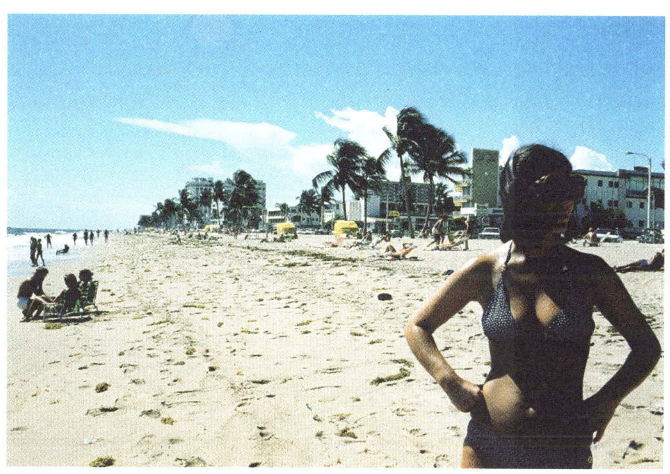

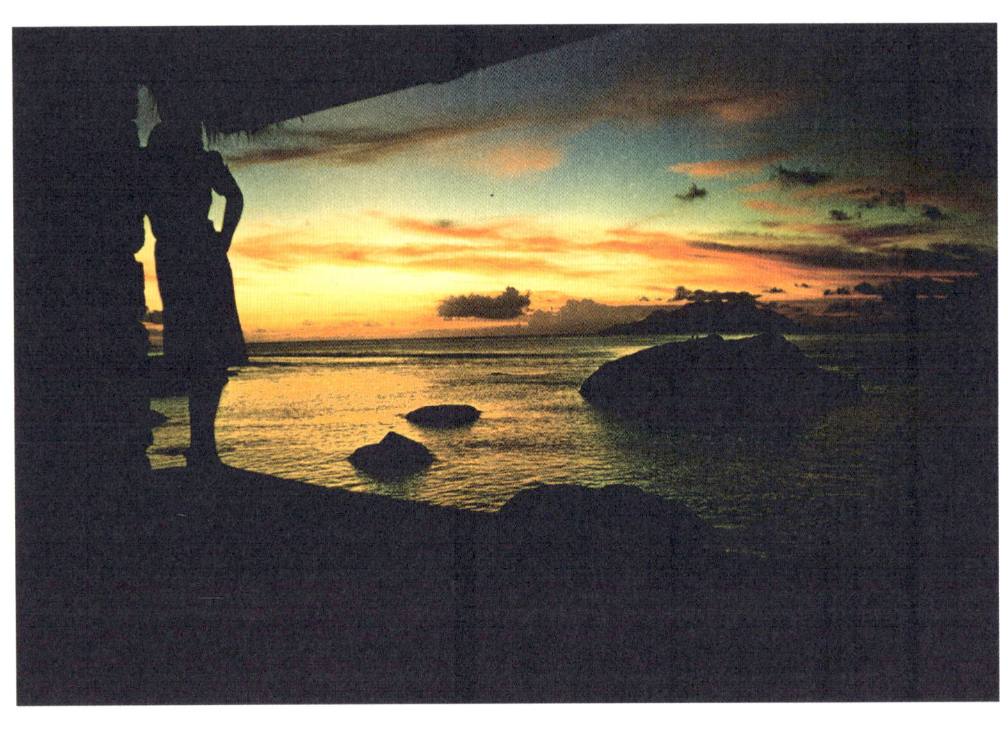

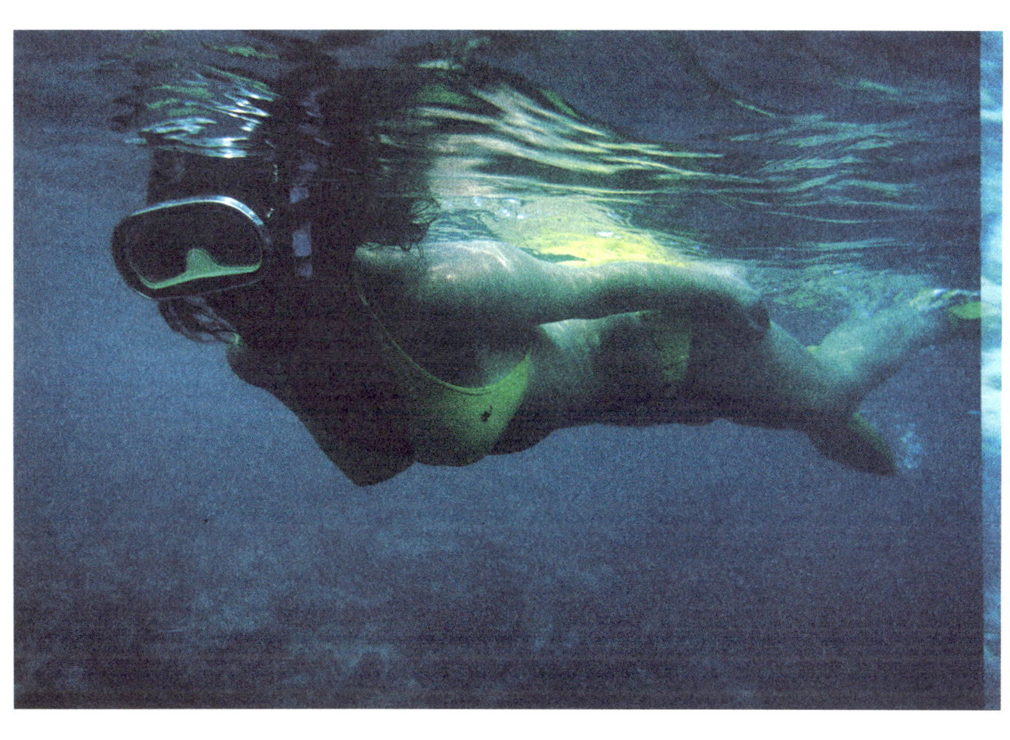

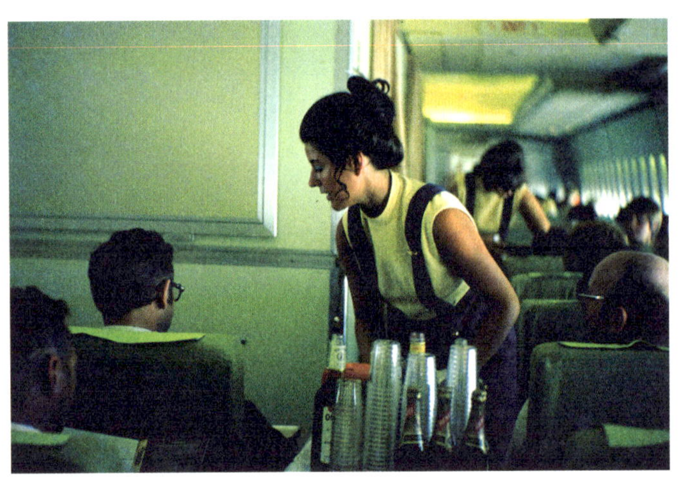

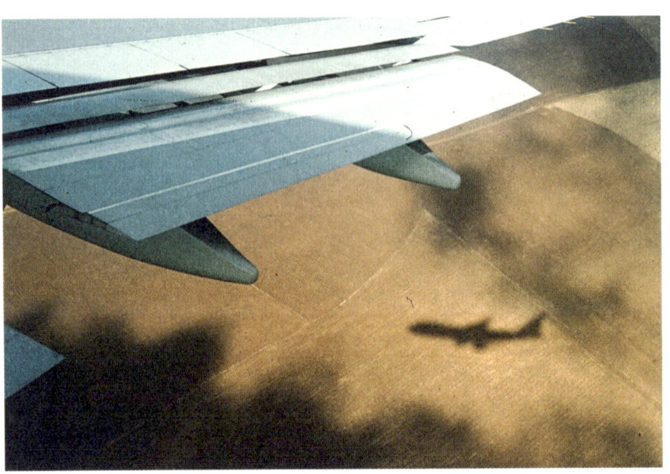

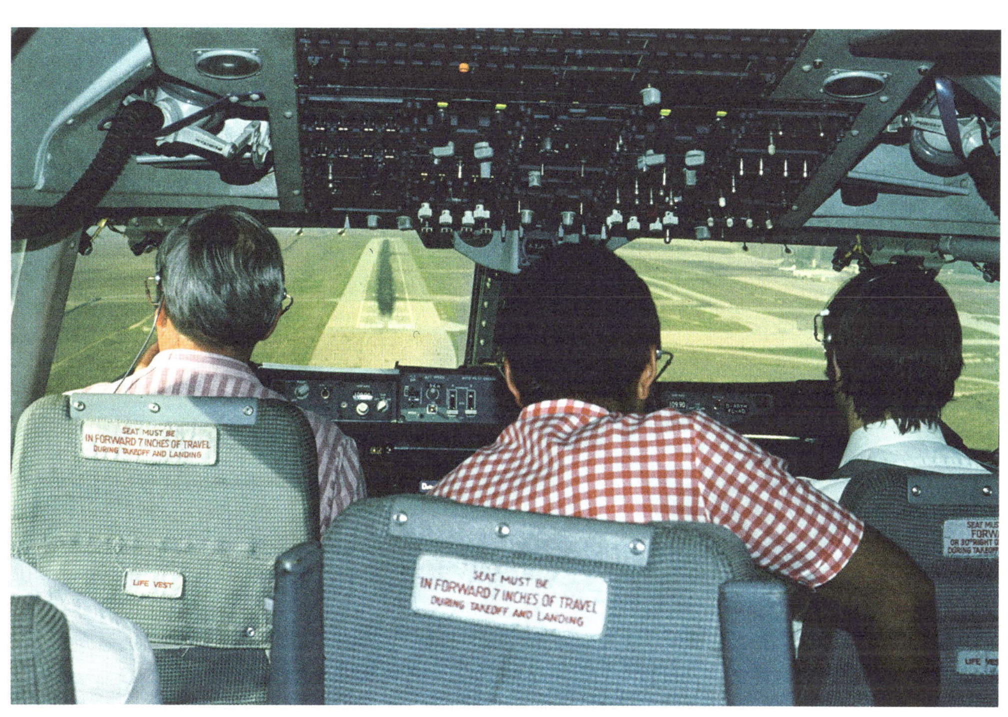
SEAT MUST BE
IN FORWARD 7 INCHES OF TRAVEL
DURING TAKEOFF AND LANDING
LIFE VEST
SEAT MUST BE
IN FORWARD 7 INCHES OF TRAVEL
DURING TAKEOFF AND LANDING

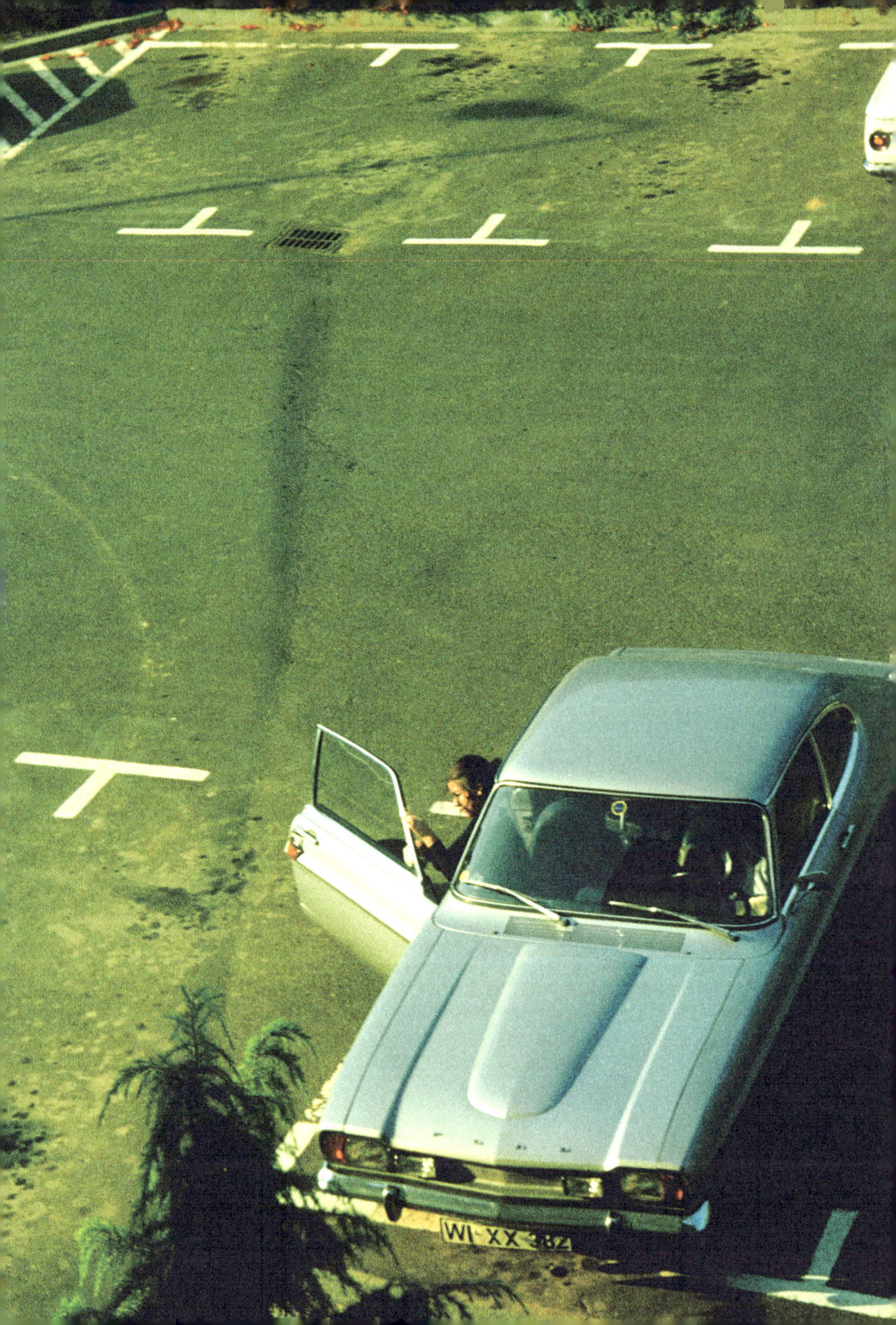
WI-XX 382

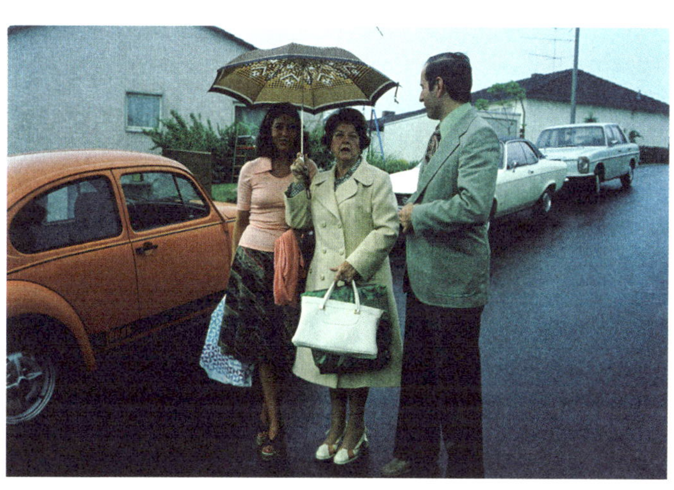

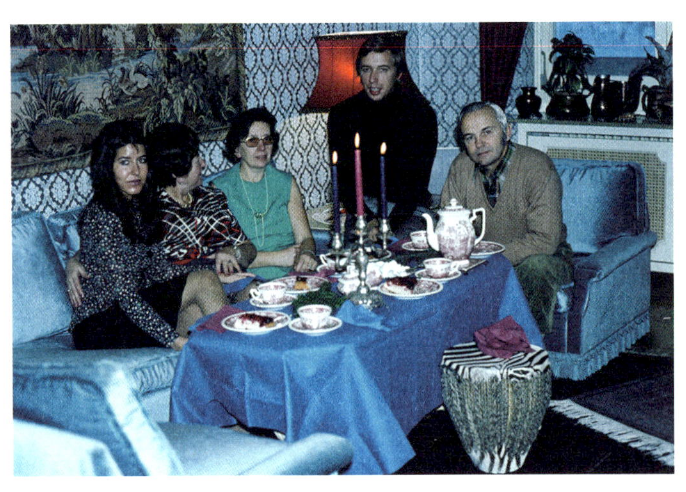

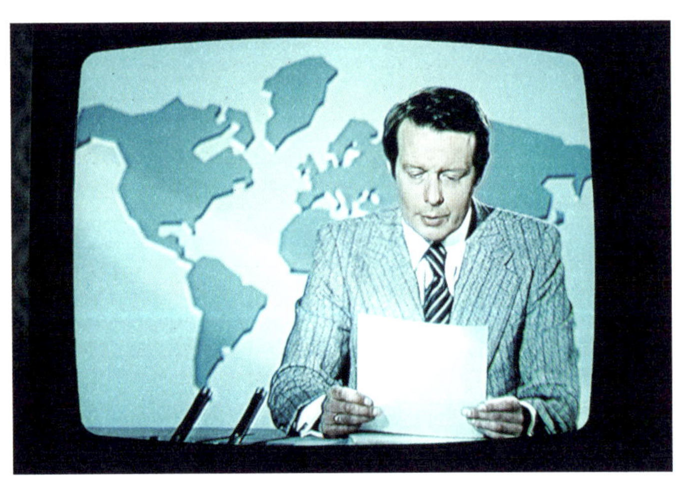

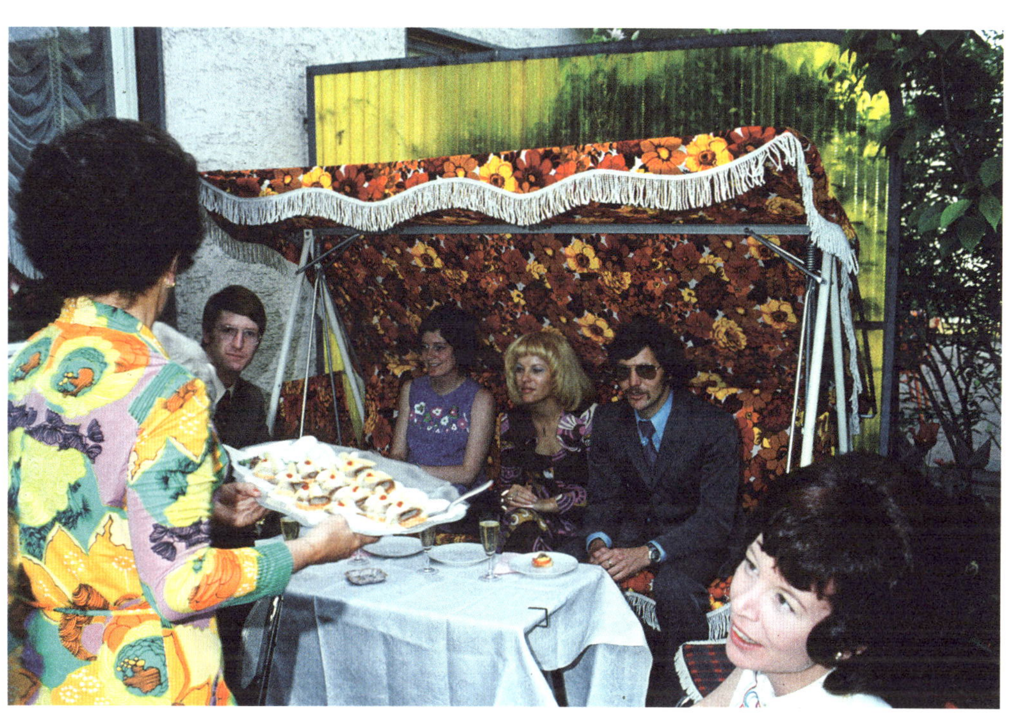

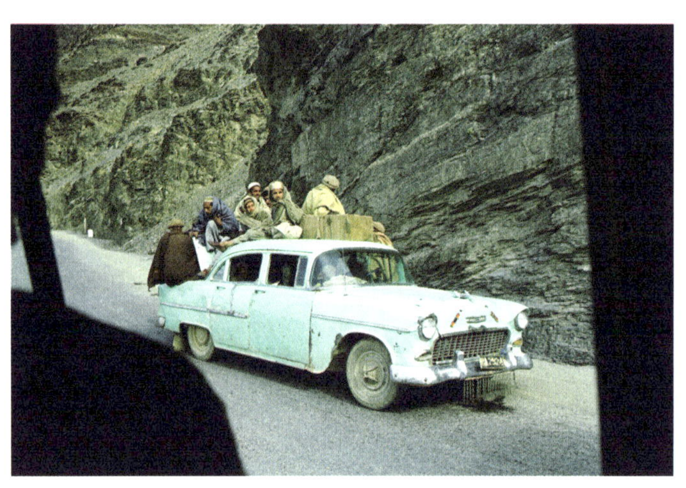

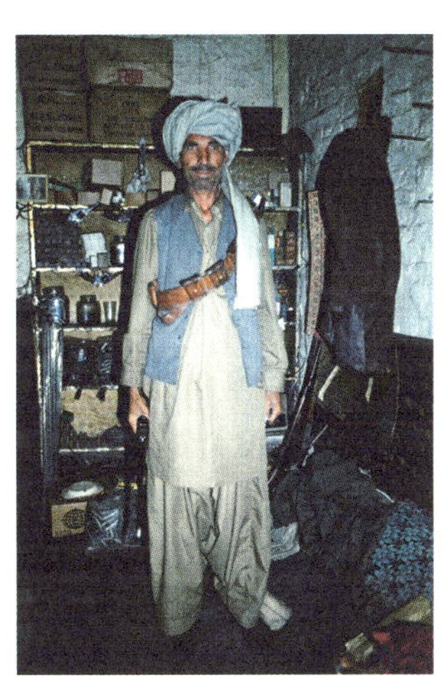

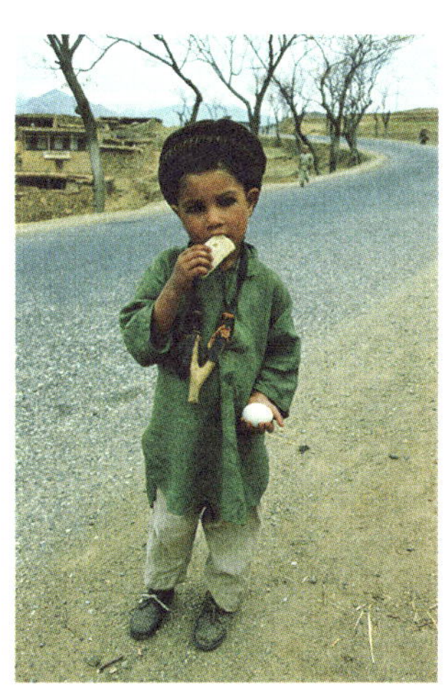

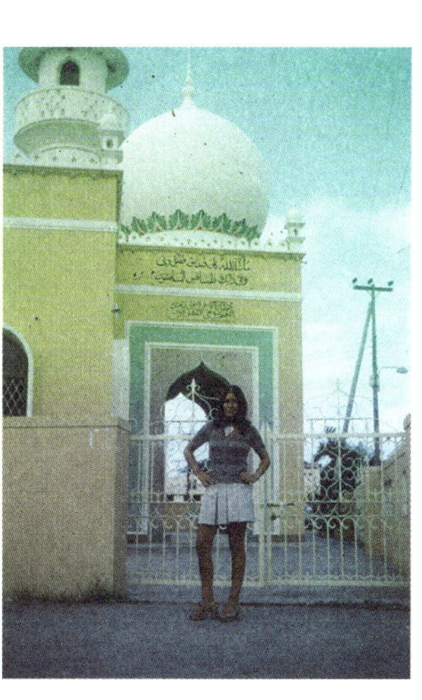

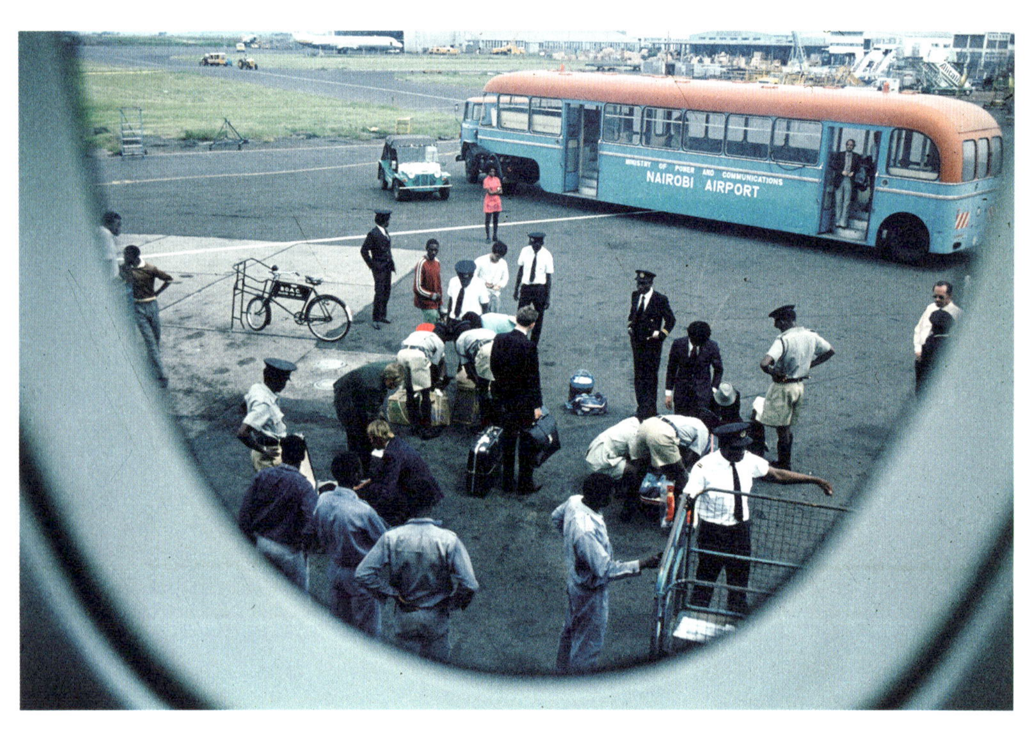
MINISTRY OF POWER AND COMMUNICATIONS
NAIROBI AIRPORT

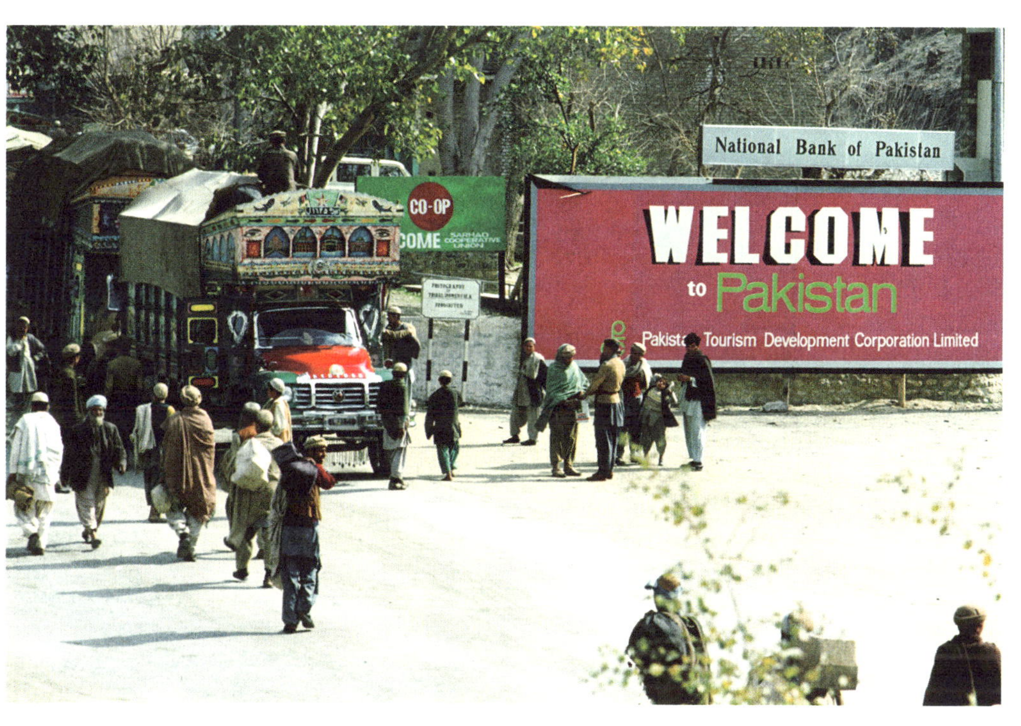
National Bank of Pakistan
CO-OP
COME
SARHAD COOPERATIVE UNION
WELCOME
to Pakistan
Pakista Tourism Development Corporation Limited

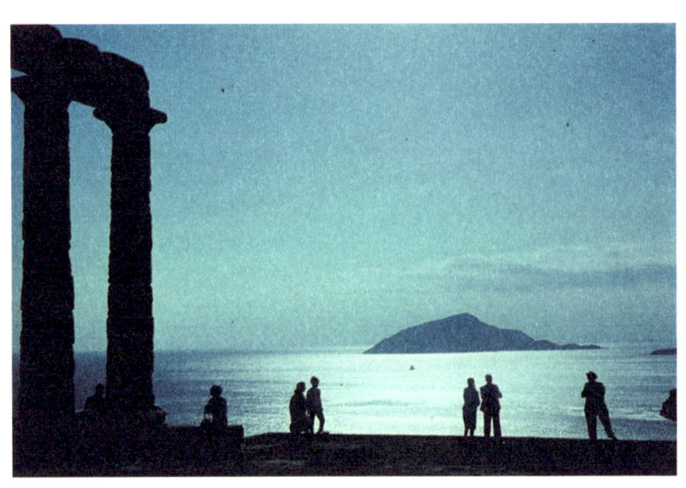

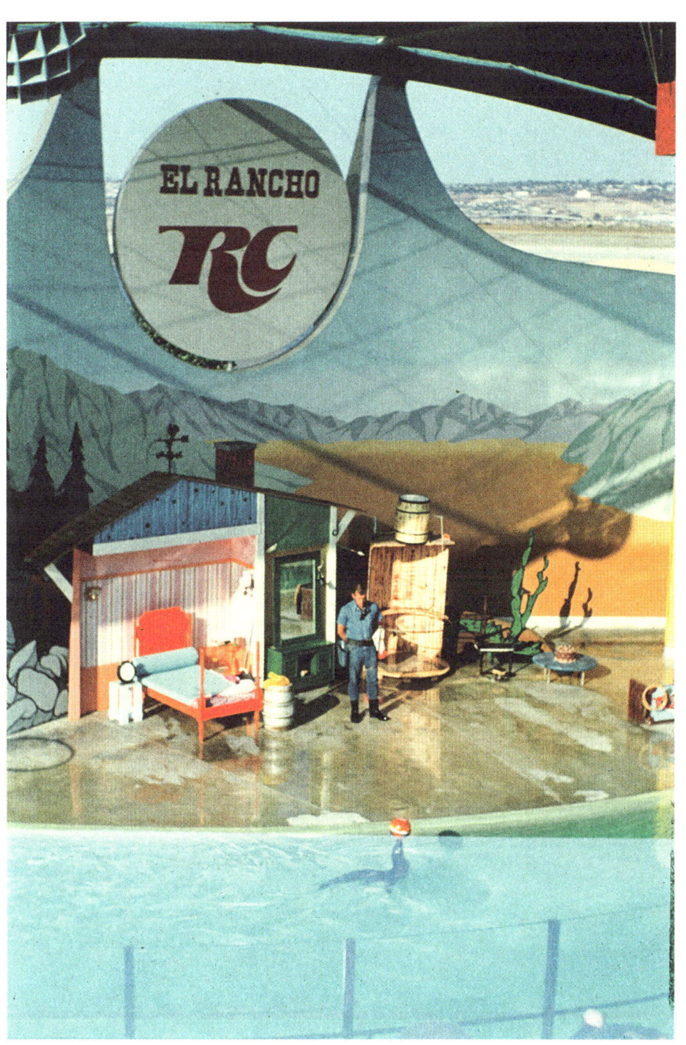
EL RANCHO
RC

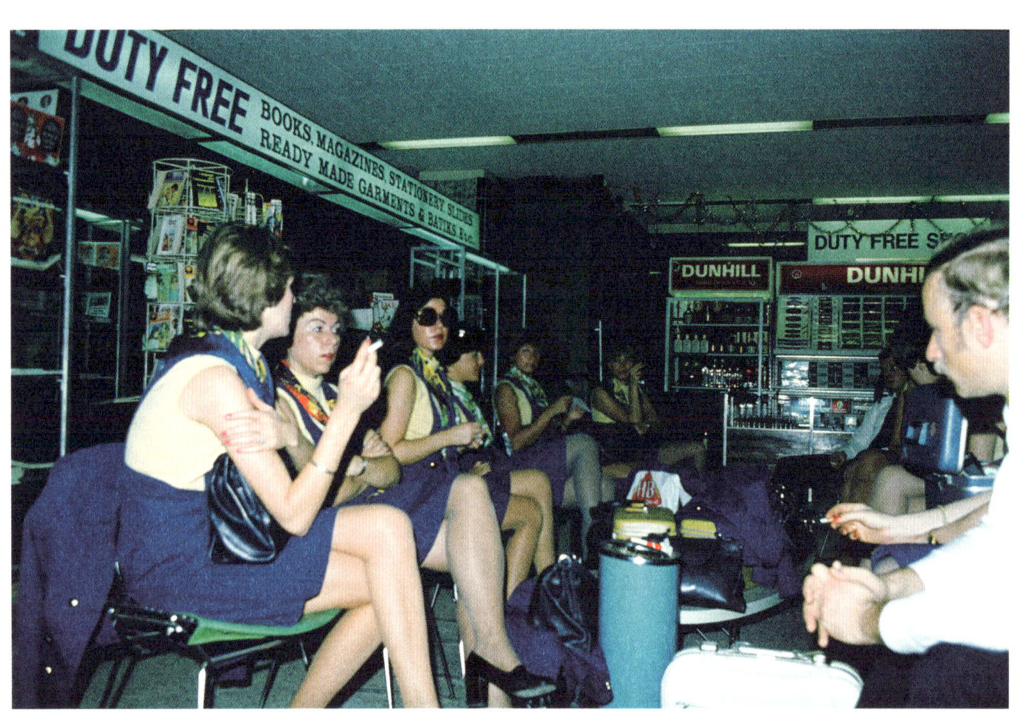
DUTY FREE
BOOKS, MAGAZINES, STATIONERY SLIDES
READY MADE GARMENTS & BATIKS Etc.
DUTY FREE
DUNHILL

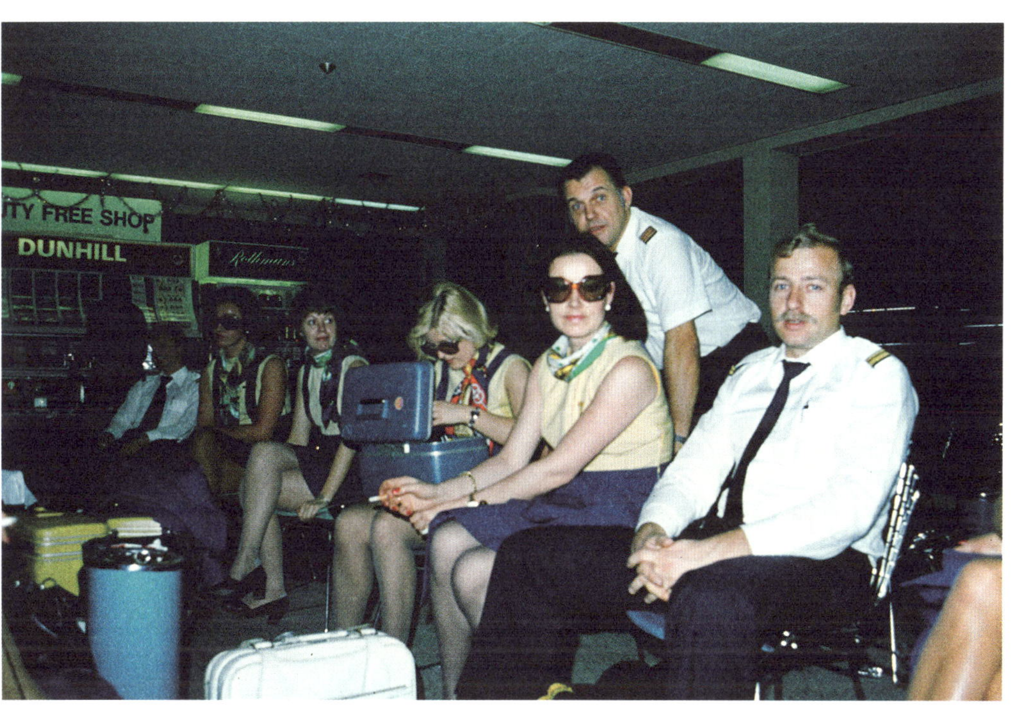
UTY FREE SHOP
DUNHILL

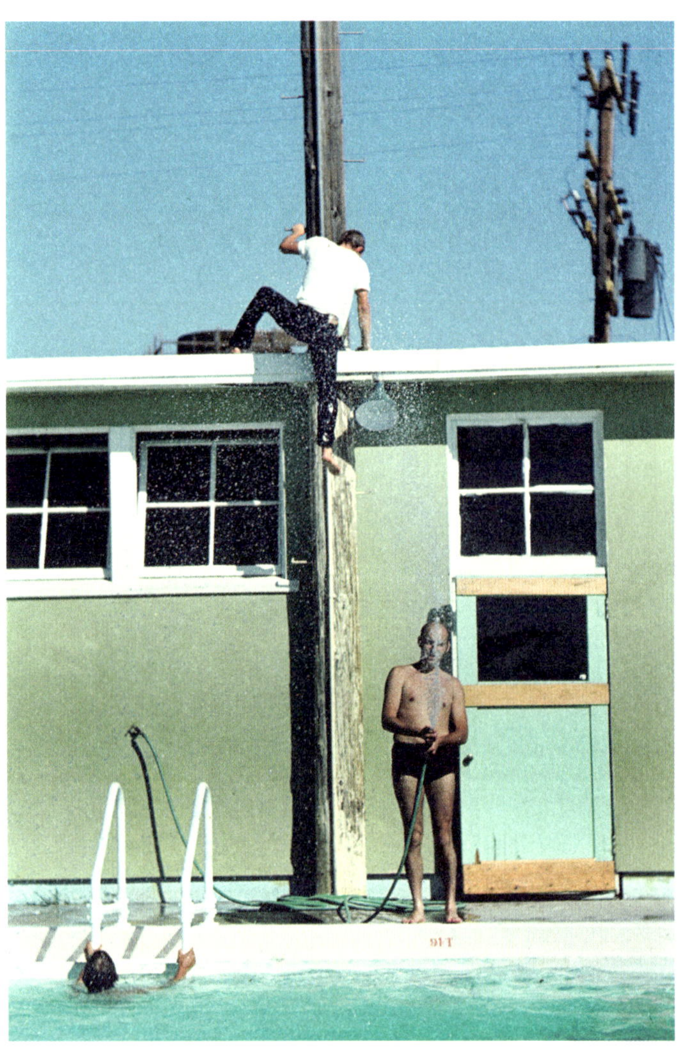

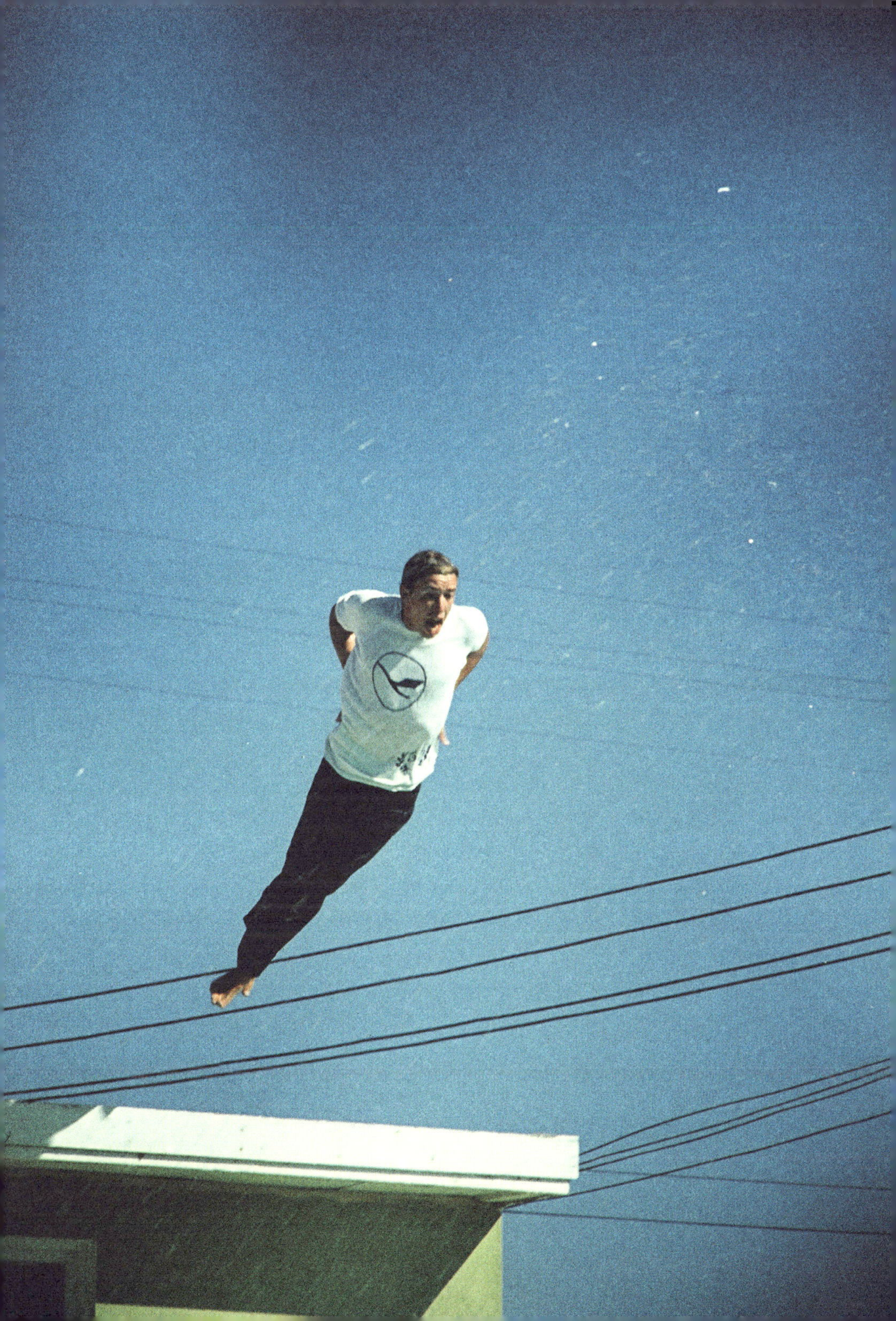

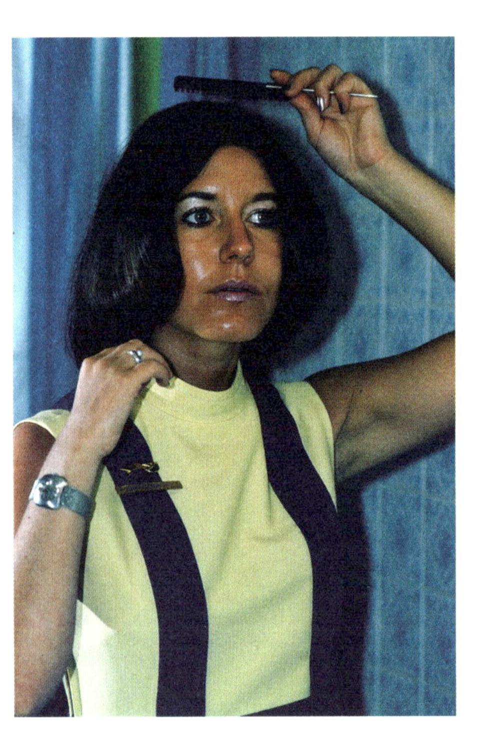

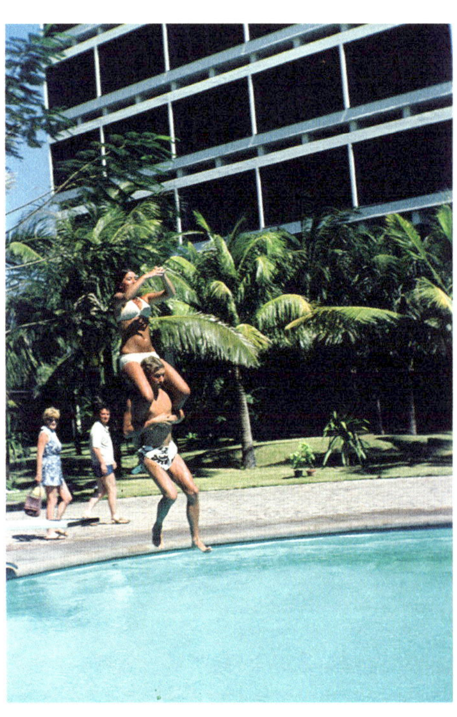

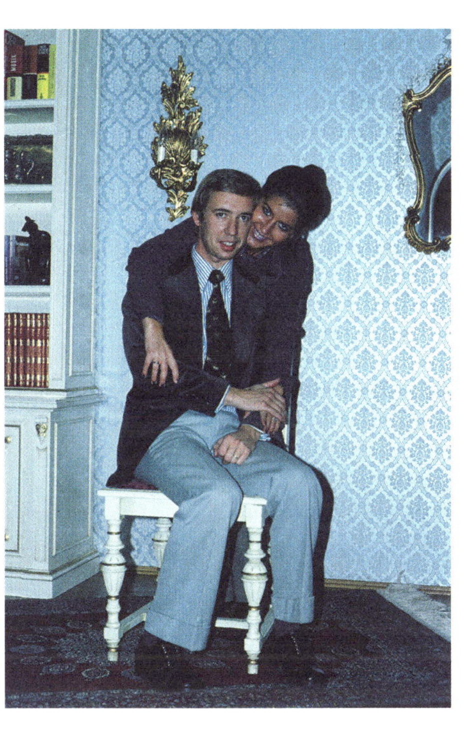

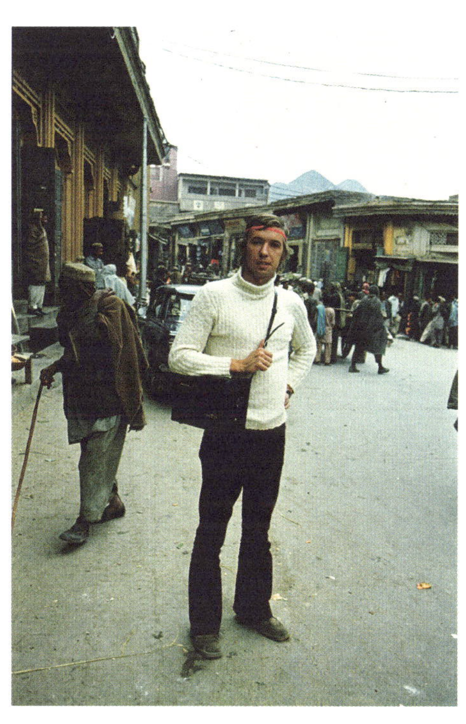

lost&found ist eine Buchreihe, in der verborgene oder verloren gegangene und wiederentdeckte Bildarchive vorgestellt werden. Sollten Sie ähnlich interessante Bilder kennen, melden Sie sich bei uns! Alle Bilder in dieser Publikation wurden nicht retuschiert.

lost&found is a book series that presents picture archives that were hidden or lost and have been rediscovered. If you are aware of similarly interesting pictures, please get in touch with us! All pictures in this publication are unretouched.

Die Publikation erscheint anlässlich der Ausstellung/This booklet is published in conjunction with the exhibition:

»Die reine Leidenschaft – Amateurfotografien von Peter Dammann, Eugen Gerbert, Axel Herrmann und Vasilii Lefter«, Opelvillen Rüsselsheim, 2. Mai – 29. Juli 2018 / May 2–July 29, 2018
www.opelvillen.de

Herausgegeben von/Edited by Beate Kemfert, Markus Hartmann

Lektorat und Übersetzung/Copyediting and translation:
Hans Georg Hiller von Gaertringen, Tas Skorupa
Gestaltung/Design: Antonia Größchen
Druck und Bindung: Druckerei Ziegler, Neckarbischofsheim
Produktion, Konzept, Verlag/Production, concept, publisher:
Hartmann Books, Rulfinger Straße 18, 70567 Stuttgart, Germany
www.hartmannprojects.com

Erste Auflage/First Edition: April 2018
Band/Volume: 4
ISBN 978-3-96070-025-8

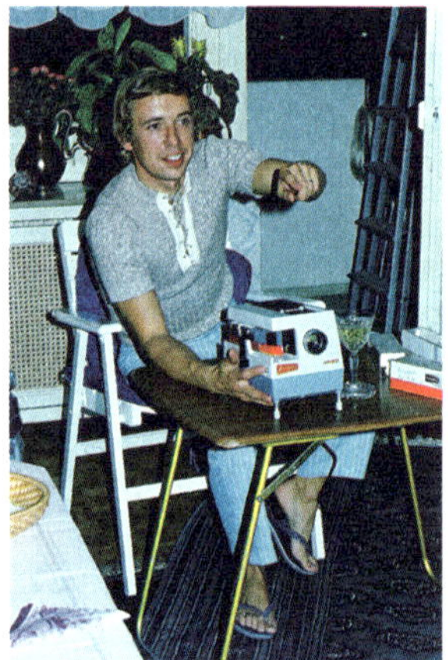

Mit freundlicher Unterstützung von/
With generous support from

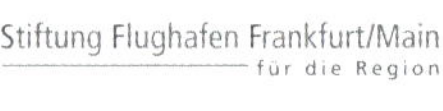

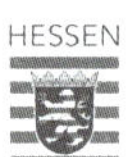